John M Bamford

The Unseen, and Song in Trial

John M Bamford

The Unseen, and Song in Trial

ISBN/EAN: 9783337019914

Printed in Europe, USA, Canada, Australia, Japan

Cover: Foto ©Thomas Meinert / pixelio.de

More available books at **www.hansebooks.com**

THE UNSEEN

AND

SONGS IN TRIAL.

THE UNSEEN,

AND

SONGS IN TRIAL.

BY

JOHN M. BAMFORD,

AUTHOR OF "THE DISCIPLE AMONG THE POOR."

London:

PUBLISHED FOR THE AUTHOR, AT THE
WESLEYAN CONFERENCE OFFICE,
2, CASTLE-STREET, CITY-ROAD;
SOLD AT 66, PATERNOSTER-ROW.

LONDON;
PRINTED BY HAYMAN BROTHERS AND LILLY,
19, CROSS ST., HATTON GARDEN, E.C.

Dedicated

TO HONOURED FRIENDS,

WHOSE CHEER AND AID WERE GIVEN

TO THE WRITER AND HIS FAMILY

IN DAYS OF TRIAL.

PREFACE.

It is a fine morning in October, and the writer has taken his seat on a tomb-stone in the churchyard of St. Tudno, situated on the Great Orme's Head, Llandudno. It seemed to him that the realm of "The Unseen," and the thoughts which are set forth in these "Songs in Trial," might find a few suitable words of introduction in this lonely and romantic spot. The stone on which he is seated is in memory of the daughter of a brother Minister, who, in the spring of her life, passed to her home in the house of her Heavenly Father; and on whose memorial stone it is written, "No night there." Close by is the old church, among whose graves thousands of visitors gathered on the fine Sunday evenings of last summer, when the service of the Church of England was conducted in the open air. But the summer is gone, and the old church is now left in its loneliness. In the winter time its solitary courts are untrodden, save by the bereaved, as they attend to bury their dead; a solemn testimony how "the fashion of this life passeth away."

The extensive view is filled in by the sea. A few small schooners are beating outside the bay; the light glinting on their sails, and presenting an emblem of man's voyage on the changing sea of human life.

For this little book the writer has to say that its contents were written during the period in which he was laid aside from active ministerial work. A vein of poetic thought was then opened in his mind, providentially, as he thinks, to save him from dwelling unhappily on an afflicted state.

Most of the pieces were composed as the writer paced the shore and rocks of Hoylake, on the Cheshire coast. He publishes them, not to earn the reputation of a poet, but for two reasons. First, in the hope that they may be a consolation to other troubled hearts, as they were to his own: and further, as a testimony of gratitude to esteemed friends, whose sympathy and succour were generously given in a time of need.

J. M. B.

LLANDUDNO,
    October, 1875.

CONTENTS.

	PAGE
The Unseen	1

SONGS IN TRIAL.

The Disabled Labourer's Dream	65
My Cross	67
The Child's Prayer and the Father's Answer	67
Sunset at Sea	69
Listen to Me	71
Active and Passive Duty	72
Trust in Christ	75
The Dying Child	76
Bells	83
Bless Me	84
Devotion	85
Devotion	86
Covenant	87
"Mors Janua Vitæ;" or, "Death the Gate of Life"	88
A Morning Hymn	93
An Evening Hymn	95
A Great Sorrow	96
O, Light is Sweet	101
The Disappointed Sower	105
The Physician's Waiting Room	109
On the Smithfield Martyrs	111
A Song	114

CONTENTS.

	PAGE
The Lord's Song	115
My Father's Grave	117
Battle	119
The Pilgrim's Night Song	122
The Angel of Hope	123
When I Feel that Life is Lonely	125
The Wounded Soldier's Outlook	126
Our Mother's Birthday	128
Rock of Ages	130
My Father, Bless Me	132
A Family Song	133
A Morning Song	135
Lord, Is it I?	136
Written for a Bereaved Mother	137
Work	139

THE UNSEEN.

THE UNSEEN.

O LEAVE me all alone,
    And let me wing my mind
Nearer the great unknown,
    That I some light may find
Into the better land which lies unseen.
    The land in which we hope
      To make our final home,
    Though in this world we grope
      For gain, and often roam
For joy, as if on earth our rest had been.

'Tis true I love the earth,
    And have no wish to leave
The rich land of my birth,
    Until I shall receive
The message of my Lord to mansions higher.
    And if Thy message come
      Sooner or later Lord,
    May I be fit for home,
      And ready for the word
Which bids me to Thy royal throne draw nigher.

O yes! the earth I love,
   Its calm majestic hills
Far towering above
   The clouds, while crystal rills
Glide down with gentle music to the vale,
  And melt into the lake
   Which glistens in the sun,
  Leaving a rippling wake
   Of wavelets as they run,
Where flocks and lowing herds their thirst regale.

I love to see the trees
   Clad in their changing robes,
And hear them in the breeze
   Waving applause to God,
As though they one and all did clap their hands.
  I love to see the flowers
   Tinted with beauty rare,
  And filling nature's bowers
   With fragrance everywhere,
Until the earthly vie with heav'nly lands.

I love the mighty sea
   When it lies smooth and calm,
As though it ne'er could be
   So angry as to harm
The hardy mariners who plough its breast.
  I love the mighty sea
   When it rolls deep and high,
  Its waves unbound and free,
   And flinging to the sky
Its frothy suds as though it ne'er would rest.

I love the grand sunrise,
   The beams of early dawn

Glowing in smiling skies
    And brightening the morn,
While song-birds in sweet carols hail the day.
    I love the calm sunset,
        When the sun-loving earth
    With tears of dew is wet,
        And hushes all its mirth
As beams the Western orb a parting ray.

    I love the early spring
        When nature bursts her chains,
And feathered warblers sing,
        In sweet and joyous strains,
Filling the woodland with their melody.
    The varied tints of grace
        Surpassing artists' skill,
Adorning earth's old face
        With virgin beauty still,
While she renews her youthful energy.

    I love the summer time,
        And yearn again to see
Nature in all her prime
        Of strength ; brimful of glee,
Glowing in ev'ry vein with buoyant health.
    Beneath bright golden skies
        From well-tilled fruitful soil
Abundant harvests rise,
        Rewarding farmers' toil
With welcome promise of her gen'rous wealth.

    I love Autumnal scenes ;
        The sweat of harvest tide ;
The thrifty cotter gleans,
        And with no little pride

Binds up her swelling sheaf and bears it home.
  Along the rural lanes,
    Between the close hedge-row
  Roll on the laden wains,
    And festoon as they go
The overhanging branches with the corn.

I love the winter too;
    Its downy flakes of snow
  Sport gaily in my view,
    And robing all below
In mantle pure such as no art could weave.
  But by the hand of God
    The precious fleece is given,
  To wrap the frozen clod
    In the kind warmth of heaven,
Till earth a fresh vitality receive.

O yes I love the earth,
    'Tis a land dear to me,
  For who can tell the worth,
    Though broken they may be,
Of the home circles which our hearts embrace?
  Where tender germs of love
    Unfold in sweetest flower,
  As in the courts above,
    More fragrant every hour,
We thus though mortal taste immortal grace.

I would give earth its due;
    'Tis not a wilderness
  Of bleak and barren hue,
    Nor clad in shattered dress
Of piercing thorns as weary pilgrims say.

'Tis not a howling waste
  Of melancholy sound,
To be passed through with haste,
  In which no joy is found,
They libel God's great work who talk this way.

It is the sinful heart
  Which is a desert drear,
Which has in Christ no part,
  No reverential fear
Of God or true submission to His will;
Perversely fumes and frets
  At every trifling pain,
And its affection sets
  On things it cannot gain,
And if it could it would be craving still.

It is the carnal mind,
  Mean, covetous, and vain,
Which to the light is blind,
  Swollen with greed of gain
And seeks no wealth save perishable gold;
Heeds not the widow's tear
  Or lonely orphan's prayer,
And when their need is near
  Goes by without a care,
And leaves them in their hunger and their cold.

Selfish it hugs its wealth
  And fain would in it trust,
Yet buys not peace or health
  But stores its gold to rust.
It would be rich but would not ever spend.
  It labours hard to get,
    But nothing has to spare,

Till caught in its own net
   And hopeless in the snare
Is claimed by Mammon, and thus comes the end.

Such minds are deserts dark,
   And joyless as the night
In which no true landmark,
   No cheerful welcome light
Meets the tired pilgrim on his weary way;
   He reaches for a staff
     But grasps a piercing thorn,
   And with a wanton laugh
     Finds all his garments torn,
And nought but rags to wear when dawns the day.

But when the heart is pure
   And cleansed from all its sin,
Of heaven's favour sure,
   Resolved its prize to win,
The promised prize which never fades away;
   When mind and strength and soul
     With Love Divine are fired,
   And grace is in the whole,
     Then man by God inspired
Enjoys true bliss, for which, O Lord, I pray.

Truly I pray for this
   And do not pray in vain,
But mingled with the bliss
   Is often chast'ning pain,
For God our Father thus doth teach His will.
   He takes the rod in hand
     But always smites in love,

That we may understand,
   As angels do above,
His pure and holy service to fulfil.

The way to future rest
   Oft lies through worldly loss,
And deeply pants the breast
   Beneath the heavy cross,
But God says "As thy days thy strength shall be."
And if the cross I bear
   With firmness till I die,
I then a crown shall wear
   Bright as the noonday sky,
Or as the stars which heaven loves to see.

'Tis true my heart doth ache
   Sometimes beneath the load,
But then for Jesu's sake
   I bear up on the road,
And He is touched with my infirmity.
The keener is the pain
   The sweeter is the balm,
I suffer but to reign,
   The storm brings near the calm,
Time's sorrows work a blest eternity.

We look at the unseen
   But with a vision dim,
A veil doth hang between,
   And yet its awful brim
Doth seem so near to earth we may look o'er.
The lamp of truth let down
   And gaze without dismay,

Heaven will never frown
   To frighten us away,
For we are heirs in Christ to all its store.

  The lamp doth freely burn
    And sheds immortal light,
  The pure celestial urn
    Our vision doth invite
Into the realm by human eye unseen;
  Not through the "gates ajar"
    Presuming glimpse to steal,
  For they wide open are
    Its glory to reveal,
And are not shut through all its day serene.

  The precious lamp I hold
    In faith's confiding hand,
  And thus Divinely bold
    Draw near the promised land,
Approach in solemn thought its outer bound
  With naked rev'rent feet
    The pearly gates I pass,
  Along the golden street
    And o'er the sea of glass,
And feel my tread to be on holy ground.

  My Father's house is there,
    There burns His gracious throne,
  And Jesus doth prepare
    Bright mansions for His own,
And buys the freehold with His precious blood;
  That their eternal right
    May be without dispute
  To dwell within His sight,
    And even hell is mute
And dares not to deny the claim is good.

O Lord I worship Thee,
    For the exceeding price
Which Thou didst pay to free
    My home in Paradise,
And give me title to it as Thine heir.
    Thank God 'tis not a lease
        Which one day may expire,
    It is eternal peace,
        My soul's supreme desire,
And God by oath my title doth declare.

    I lift the lamp on high,
        And love the blessed ray
    Which reaches the pure sky
        Of never waning day:
Thus while it gives me light may I receive
    From heaven's Holy One,
        The unction of His grace,
    To help a finite son
        To look upon the face
Of God, and saints, and further joys perceive.

    O have I dared to ask
        Jehovah's face to see?
    When even those who bask
        In immortality
Their persons veil, and Holy, Holy, cry.
    If I have asked too much
        My sovereign Lord forgive,
    And let Thy gracious touch
        Now bid my spirit live,
While in Thy royal presence I draw nigh.

    Still, Lord, Thine ear incline,
        Veil with another fold,

Thy glory doth outshine,
  Thy smile I now behold,
Love is of all Thine attributes the sum.
  Uphold me while I gaze,
    Or my weak heart will melt
  In Deity's bright blaze,
    For I Thy love have felt
To be "the power of the world to come."

  The sum! Who can it count?
    What fathom line can sound
  The great Eternal Fount?
    It is a deep profound
Which neither men nor angels can explore.
  Infinite in the past
    Before the birth of time,
  And shall for ever last
    In its primeval clime
Without decay when time shall be no more.

  It flows without a shore
    And yet I sail its sea,
  No tongue can tell its store
    Yet it belongs to me;
I am unworthy e'en to wet my lip
  At such a spring as this,
    And yet may drink until
  My heart o'erflows with bliss,
    And thus my joy may fill
At the pure stream which I've no right to sip.

  And yet I have a right
    Which in Love's bosom lies,
  Beams of Eternal light
    Now print it in the skies,
For tis no secret, God doth make it known.

THE UNSEEN.

He graves my filial name
   Upon His royal hand,
That heav'n may see my claim
   True as Himself to stand,
And firm as the foundations of His throne.

Emboldened by the grace
   Which is so freely given,
I look into the face
   Of Christ my Lord in heaven,
And there I mirrored see Love's glory shine.
   So strong and full and bright,
     The medium of the cross
   Is needful to my sight,
     That in its pain and loss
I may both see and feel the Love Divine.

O what a lense of light
   The cross supplies to me,
I look into the might
   Of Christ's divinity:
In grateful meditation I adore.
   My vision seems to swell
     Heav'n's vast expanse to take,
   As if a pebble fell
     Into a calm deep lake
And rolls its central ripples to the shore.

Full in my mental view
   I see a temple fair,
Immortal light shines through,
   And God Himself is there
Robed in the grandeur of eternity.
   Behold! a burning throne!
     And seven lamps of fire

THE UNSEEN.

Brighter than sun e'er shone,
  Glow with intense desire,
For they are Spirits of the Deity.

  The temple vast is filled
    With God's majestic train,
  Its radiance doth gild
    The temple o'er again,
And sheds its glory to the lofty dome.
  The swift-winged lightnings flash
    From the Almighty's seat,
  The deep-toned thunders crash
    Beneath His sovereign feet,
And echo downwards where lost spirits roam.

  But the dread throne is spanned
    As by the em'rald bow
  Streaming from God's right hand,
    His attributes to show
In perfect harmony with Love Divine:
  Within its warm embrace
    Mercy and Truth unite,
  And Justice crowned with Grace
    Shines forth in purest light,
To heav'n and earth a holy cov'nant sign.

  I come to Zion's mount
    By faith, and see the crowd
  Of angels at the Fount
    Of Life, who cry aloud
The praise of God, and veiling, lowly bend:
  The church of the first-born;
    The spirits of the just,
  Clad as the sons of morn,
    And Jesus whom they trust,
And I trust too, my Saviour and my Friend.

Around the lofty seat
  Of High Divinity,
Father, Son, and Spirit,
  The Holy Trinity,
The white-robed elders in their crowns of gold
  Partake of regal state,
    As minor priests and kings ;
  How glorious and great
    The countless gatherings
From every part of Heaven's eternal fold.

Abraham tried and sad
  When toiling up Moriah,
To offer the loved lad
  With sacrificial fire,
Who well enquired, "Where is the chosen lamb?"
  The altar firmly piled,
    And hushed the heartfelt strife,
  The father took his child
    And stretched aloft the knife,
But God said " Loose thy son and slay the ram."

Thus tried and proved he won
  Distinction which remained
In his beloved son,
  And his son's son retained ;
God doth their royal heritage ordain.
  Their names like links of gold
    In patriarchal line,
  Their memories enrolled
    Within the Church Divine,
And never shall die out while God doth reign.

Near to the central throne
  My faith beholds with awe,

Him who from God alone
    Received the moral law,
And gazed upon Jehovah from the clift:
    From Sinai's rugged brow
        He bore the tables down:
    Honour and glory now
        Shine in the splendid crown
He took on Pisgah's top as God's free gift.

    I trace a burnished track
        Right through the gates of pearl;
    It throws my vision back
        To see the chariot whirl
Which bore Elijah to his Master's throne:
    The royal charioteer
        Reined in his steeds of fire,
    Out stepped the faithful seer,
        Who proving Baal a liar,
Cried, "If the Lord be God serve Him alone."

    Unharnessed, the swift steeds
        Rest in the royal stud,
    Ready for other deeds
        Of transport, if it should
Be God's great will to send them forth again.
    If He but speak the word
        The fire steeds take the yoke,
    Obey Jehovah's curb
        As when of old He spoke;
The signal given, it shall be now as then.

    David whose harp is fired
        With perfect harmony,
    Whose skilful hand inspired
        With sweeter melody
Than ever charmed the evil heart of Saul:

THE UNSEEN.

His fingers on the string,
    Ready to swell the strain
In honour of the King
    Who over all doth reign,
And his rare art engage at heaven's call.

Isaiah, too, is there,
    Intense with hallowed flame,
To take seraphic share
    In homage of the name
Which cherubim continually praise.
    Full of poetic thought
        As living waters roll;
    To tell what God hath wrought
        The Spirit moves his soul,
Until it flows as a pure stream of grace.

The gifted Jeremiah,
    The anguish of whose mind
Was like a pent-up fire;
    So earnestly he pined
To make men hear what God had bade him say.
    No wail of human pain
        Breaks from his spirit now;
    His tears which fell like rain
        Ne'er soil his noble brow,
For God's own hand hath wiped them all away.

Daniel the brave and true,
    Who feared the lions less,
Or what fierce men could do
    Who hard decrees would press,
Than to disown his Lord, the King of kings.
    If he had shunned the den
        And thus dishonoured God,

The scorn of mocking men,
  Jehovah's angry rod,
And conscience, would have lashed him with
    their stings.

A long and noble line
  Of Prophets, Priests and Kings,
Illustrious they shine,
  Enriched with heav'nly things
Beyond all monarchies of human pride.
  With royalty adorned
    Than God's alone less dim,
  Now sanctified and formed
    In glory like to Him
The Lord of all, and seated by His side.

The apostolic saints
  In close communion,
No jealousy attaints
  Their bond of union,
On twelve high thrones they sit near to their
    Lord :
Their lives not counted dear,
  But poured out for the sake
Of Him whom they revere.
  By axe, or cross, or stake
They sealed with their own blood the precious
    word.

The mother of our Lord
  Moves in the holy scene,
Not there to be adored
  As an immortal queen,
But blessed for her love to Him she bore.
  She loved Him as a child,
    She loved Him as a man,

She loved Him when reviled,
   And when His life blood ran,
The spikes which pierced the Son the mother tore.
  Strong in her mother's might
    But stronger in her Son's,
  Her faith obtained a right
    Among His precious ones,
And her heart to her Son's did closely bind.
  Thus filled with Love's true pow'r
    She sat beneath His cross
  In Calvary's dread hour,
    Unconscious that her loss
Was the redeeming gain of all mankind.

  Type of a mother true,
    And virtuous and wise,
  Good women not a few
    Have sought a kindred prize
In Jesu's love, and have not sought in vain.
  High in the temple throng
    They radiantly shine,
  With grace they move among
    The saints, and still entwine
Their holy virtues round their loved again.

  But what are these I see,
    Who in the temple wait
  So lovingly and free
    Amid the regal state,
And rev'rend gravity of elders round?
  O what are these so bright
    And beautiful and fair,
  Glancing like beams of light
    And sweeter than the rare
Perfumes of earthly fragrance ever found?

Has the Almighty King
   Preserved and choicer lands,
From which He thus doth bring
   The culture of His hands
To bud His people's pleasures with His own?
   Are these the plants of prize,
     Which angels love to rear
   In bow'rs of Paradise,
     And by all heav'n held dear,
From the great Lord to each before His throne?

Nay these more precious are
   Than plants of finest hue,
Of greater value far
   Than flow'rs we ever knew,
These are the children of Eternity:
   Permitted now to gaze
     Into their Father's face,
   And happy in the blaze
     Of the pure throne of grace,
They win the loving smiles of Deity.

When doting mothers brought
   The children to their Lord,
And in affection sought
   For them a gracious word,
He took them in His arms and kindly blest:
   And now on Zion's hill
     His heart is just the same,
   He loves the children still
     Revealing His great name
To their expanding minds in saintly rest.

What tongue can tell the charm
   These little ones of love

Spread o'er the sacred calm
   Of the dear home above?
They're ev'rywhere, and ev'rywhere they seem
   Like a bright fringe of gold
     To the great witness cloud,
   Among the saints of old
     Their voices sound aloud,
As the sweet rippling of a silver stream.

   They to the temple come
     And vast their numbers be,
   But God hath made them room
     In His large family,
Nor suffers them to range in ranks obscure:
   He bids them with delight
     Their holy freedom take,
   And in His nearer sight
     Enjoy for Jesu's sake
Their full capacity among the pure.

   As in the midst of ocean
     Far out of sight of land,
   The vast congregation
     Extends on ev'ry hand,
Or like a bright and star-lit firmament.
   Who can survey its range
     Or who its numbers tell?
   And yet it is not strange
     For many I love well
Are there with whom I've oft held covenant.

   Hear now the ceaseless cry
     Of flaming seraphim,
   "Jehovah, Lord Most High,
     For ever unto Him,
The Holy, Holy, Holy be all praise."

Clearly their voices blend
    The temple vast to fill,
The worshippers attend
    With one harmonious will,
And not a thought in their pure homage strays.

No other voice is heard,
    One voice proclaims "The Holy,"
No other sound is stirred,
    All sounds proclaim His glory:
The cry floats in an awful silence still.
The universe seems hushed
    To listen to His name,
And even heaven is flushed
    To realize its gain
In the fruition of so pure a will.

The heavens can't contain
    The holiness of God,
The virtue of His name
    And mandate of His rod
No limit have, but without bound extend
From heaven to the earth,
    From angels unto men;
May grace bring to the birth
    More saintly sons, and then
Help them to keep the faith unto the end.

"Holy, Holy, Holy,"
    The white robed elders all
Responsively and lowly
    Before Jehovah fall,
Who liveth in eternity sublime.
Each elder casteth down
    Before the royal throne

His priceless golden crown,
　　　　Crying, "O God alone
"Thou art unreckoned by the note of time."

"Worthy O God Thou art,
　　　Honour is due to Thee,
　　Let every creature part
　　　With all its vanity,
And know it lives by Thine almighty will.
　　Thou dost all life create,
　　　Thou dost all things sustain,
　　On Thee all creatures wait,
　　　And never wait in vain,
All need in heaven and earth Thou dost fulfil."

　　A silent interlude
　　　Of still solemnity,
　　And now the multitude
　　　With loud immensity
Of voice;—yet all melodious, exclaim,
　"Salvation to our God,
　　　Salvation to the Lamb
　　Who washed us in His blood,
　　　And sealed us with His name,
Redeemed us from our sin, its curse and shame.

"From ev'ry land we came
　　　But all united here,
　　All sealed with one great name,
　　　All by the Lamb held dear;
One Head: one home, one family we are.
　　No discord spoils our peace,
　　　No jealousy we feel;
　　In love we all increase,
　　　Nor foe shall ever steal
Our holy charity, our oneness mar.

" We look into the heart
  Of Deity supreme,
But there we find no part
  With those who would redeem
A few elect, and leave out all the rest.
  Jehovah's heart is great,
    All tribes and tongues takes in,
  And there they learn to mate
    As brethren of one kin,
For love blends all distinctions in its breast.

" We were condemned and lost,
    But He our ransom paid,
  His precious life it cost,
    On Him our help was laid,
And in omnipotence He bore it all;
  Death smote Him with his dart
    And Satan bruised His heel,
  And in His stricken heart
    An agony did feel;
So great our wilful sin, so deep our fall.

" To slaughter He was led
    Though innocent and pure,
  He bowed His holy head
    The death blow to endure,
And gave His soul an offering for sin.
  It pleased the great I AM
    To save His sheep astray,
  By wounding the loved Lamb
    Which in His bosom lay,
And thus provide a fold to take them in.

" They gave Him gall to drink
    Upon a soldier's reed,

They mocked His great life sink
  And gloried in the deed :
But in redeeming mercy thus He prayed,
 ' Father forgive them all,
  They know not what they do,
O hear My dying call,
  For though with scorn they view
The travail of My soul ; for them it's paid.'

" Now save Thyself they cried
  And come down from the tree ;
His agony replied,
 ' Hast Thou forsaken Me ?
My God, My God, why leave Me thus alone ? '
  O saints and angels all
How wonderful His grace,
  Our tears of love still fall
While we behold His face,
For yet He bears the scars upon His throne.

" They laid Him in the rock
  And sealed the massive stone,
They fain His strength would lock
  In the dark grave alone,
But never key was found the bolt to roll.
  They set the bravest guard
And charged them have a care,
  The task was very hard
Almighty power was there ;
They slew His body, but touched not His soul.

" The powers of hell He spoiled,
  Disarmed death of his sting,
The tempter's craft He foiled
  And crippled his dark wing ;
He fought the dreadful battle and He won.

Upon the dragon's head
  He planted His bruised heel,
Our foe a captive led
  And bound him with His seal,
And to His feet all enemies shall come.

" Salvation to our God,
  Who gave His precious Son,
He suffered not the clod
  Defile His Holy One ;
Corruption craved its prey, but craved in vain.
  The resurrection life
    Of His redeeming plan
  Dispelled the mortal strife,
    And now the Son of Man
Holds the strong keys of Death and Hell's domain.

" O death where is thy sting ?
  Thy victory O grave ?
The Conqueror doth bring
  Through thee His power to save ;
O death, O grave, thy work will soon be o'er :
  Thy strength He will destroy,
    Thy prey He will unclose,
  His own shall rise with joy,
    And over all His foes
His triumph shall maintain for evermore.

" In mediatorial care
  He rose from Bethany,
The regal throne to share
  In filial Deity ;
Ascending to His royal Father's side.
  Sound of His princely tread
    Called heaven forth to greet

The first fruits of the dead,
    And escort to the seat,
Of sov'reign love this sheaf of harvest-tide.

"Triumphant legions cried,
    Lift up your heads, O gates,
  Droop not for Him that died,
    The King of Glory waits
Admission in the fulness of His power.
  Who is this mighty King
    In robes of crimson hue,
  Who doth such honour bring
    And claim such homage due,
Demanding His pure Bride and her rich dower?

"He is the Lord of Hosts,
    Who hath on Calvary
  Paid man's redemption costs,
    And crowned with victory,
He captive leads in His triumphant train
  The last of all His foes,
    Death staggers on to die
  While his great Conqueror goes
    To Majesty on High,
In everlasting monarchy to reign.

"O gates! your portals raise
    A fruitful sheaf we bring,
  With universal praise
    To our Creator King,
Than gold or pearls a sheaf of richer grain.
  O gates! your breadth expand,
    The reapers will bring more
  Sheaves to the King's right hand,
    Until the royal store
A wealth of immortality contain.

"We look on death's domain
    Which in corruption lies,
  But quick with life again
    The mortal seed shall rise,
Broadcast 'tis sown, and broadcast it shall spring.
  In every lonesome grave,
    And in the deepest sea
  Beneath the rolling wave
    All vital it shall be,
When the last trump of the great day shall ring.

"In weakness it is sown,
    It shall be raised in power,
  The earth receives its own
    But for time's fleeting hour,
The incorruptible must be put on.
  From every Christian tomb
    Held by our Lord in trust,
  Immortal life shall bloom
    Out of the mortal dust,
In the pure glory of the Holy One.

"The harvest draweth near
    And angel-reapers stand,
  Waiting the word to shear
    With sickles in their hand,
The Sheaf of Promise hath already come.
  Bereaved weep o'er their graves
    And linger mourning still,
  But see! the harvest waves,
    And soon on Zion's hill
Heaven shall be merry in its harvest home.

"O that our joyful song
    May reach our friends below,

Who think of us and long
   More perfectly to know
The everlasting blessedness we feel.
  'Tis theirs, the dead to weep,
   'Tis ours, their life to sing,
All who in Jesus sleep
   He will most surely bring
To rest where mortal wounds shall sweetly heal.

" 'Tis theirs, with friends to part,
   'Tis ours, with them to meet,
Bereavement fills their heart,
   Ours, with warm welcome greet,
They see them leave, but we do take them in.
  'Tis theirs, to see the wave
   Of swelling Jordan's storm,
  'Tis theirs, to close the grave
   Upon the mortal form,
They see the strife, but we the crown they win.

" They see the human brain,
   Yielding its feeble powers
  Beneath the mortal strain
   In time's swift ebbing hours,
As if the soul itself was weak and dim.
  We see the human mind
   Expanding in the sun
  Of Christ's pure love, and find
   The greatness He hath won
For them in nearer fellowship with Him.

" They say, 'Thy will be done'
   With many bitter tears,
  They, too, adore the Son,
   But oft with doubts and fears ;
We know the way of trial that they come ;

For we have paced it too
  With bruised and tire-worn feet,
But God hath brought us through
  To His eternal seat,
Where sighs and sorrows are for ever done.

"O could our brethren hear
  The beating of our wing,
While ministering near
  To guard them while they cling
To the great Rock of Ages cleft in twain.
  The heart Divine is filled
    With kindred sympathy,
  And on His love they build
    In their infirmity
A friendly refuge, and a shelter gain.

"O may His grace sustain
  Our brethren in the way,
Help them to bear the pain
  Until the break of day,
When the long night of weeping shall be o'er.
  Fain would we drop the balm
    Into their wounded breast,
  But the almighty arm
    Shall bear them on to rest
In the safe haven of this peaceful shore.

"We the hard fight have won,
  And they shall win it too,
We have received our crown,
  And theirs is now in view,
The righteous Judge hath laid it up in store.
  Ere long we shall embrace
    Our friends who toil below,

THE UNSEEN.

With Jesus face to face
    No pain or parting know ;
Sin shall not soil or sever any more.

" Now let the chorus ring
    Like a clear clarion blast,
Till unbelief shall bring
    Its evidence at last,
And fools who have denied with shame confess. .
  Sweet may the chorus sound
    To all who now believe,
And as on holy ground
    Its harmony receive,
O while they listen may Jehovah bless.

" Loud let the chorus swell
    And fill the universe,
Until the powers of hell
    In terror shall disperse
Behind the rocking gates of their stronghold.
  Angels and saints unite,
    And seraphim still cry
With melody and might
    Until all worlds reply,
And chaos wakes to hear the anthem rolled.

" Our voice shall reach the lost
    In their deep, dark despair,
That they may know the cost
    Of Christ's redeeming care,
Which they, alas! so wilfully despised.
  Justice hath shut the door
    With Mercy's full consent,
No hope for evermore
    That Jesus will relent,
His acts are true and ne'er can be revised.

" Beelzebub shall know
    That all are loyal here,
  Now let our ancient foe
    Hearken to us with fear,
His chain is forged and soon he shall be bound.
  Behold the angel stand
    With the great key of hell,
  And in his mighty hand
    The fetters welded well,
Waiting God's will to bind the foe aground.

" The *bottomless* is deep,
    The dragon fierce and bold,
  But down the fearful steep
    He shortly shall be rolled,
And in its lowest depths shall be enchained.
  He shall deceive no more,
    But writhe beneath the seal
  Which chafes his spirit sore,
    And curbs his evil zeal,
Forbidding him the kingdom he hath gained.

" Sound! ye angelic choirs,
    Lift up your harps on high,
  Sound! for the Lord inspires,
    And holy seraphs cry,
Sound! ye His saints the song of the redeemed.
  Sound! in the Church below,
    Let earth combine with heaven
  In harmony to show
    The grace which God hath given,
Sound all! our theme is by the King esteemed."

* * * * * * * *

  Hark! hark! the chorus swells
    In a grand minstrelsy,

Its triumph boldly tells
   Like the deep booming sea,
As waves on waves gather their awful sound ;
   Till the whole ocean roars
      With all its might and main
   Upon its trembling shores,
      But dies away again,
And whispers faintly in the vast profound.

Or as a thunder peal
   Crashes among the hills,
And shakes them to the keel :
   Their throbbing bosom fills
With throes of travail which asunder tear,
   Till hoary rocks are riven ;
      Yet soon it floats away
   Into the vault of heaven,
      But lingers in its play
While smitten nature soothes its tempest care.

It comes ! with startling roll,
   As if a mighty world
Were split from pole to pole,
   And its huge fragments hurled
In chaos depths which echo back the fall ;
   Now melts in sweetest strains
      Of music soft and clear,
   That e'en Jehovah deigns
      To bend a list'ning ear,
Delighting in the Lamb as all in all.

The harps are sounding now,
   And harpers sweetly sing,
With light upon their brow
   And life in ev'ry string,
A countless host of lyres and all inspired ;

Full of the breath Divine
    And played with finest skill :
May one of these be mine
    To praise my Father's will,
Tuned by the love with which all heaven is fired.

Hath melody its strings
    Vocal in every sphere ?
Do all created things
    The Lamb of God revere,
And take appointed part to bless His name ?
    God's omnipresent hand
        Touches all springs of life,
    And at His just command
        E'en hell in its deep strife,
A base of harmony adds in its shame.

The heaven of heavens is filled,
    And earth and air and seas,
And ev'ry creature thrilled
    With the harmonious breeze
Which stirs the immeasurable universe ;
    Bearing the honour due
        To Him, amidst the throne,
    And in His royal view
        To Him, and Him alone,
Yea every knee doth bow and tongue confess.

Eternity's vast shore,
    Lined with ten thousand times
Ten thousand saints and more,
    Rings out its joyful chimes,
And the grand chorus rises in full tone.
    O hear its mighty voice,
        The theme it doth declare.

Rejoice! my heart rejoice!
　　Thou hast a humble share
In the pure joy which swells up to the throne.

" O worthy is the Lamb
　　That was on Calv'ry slain,
　The pure eternal Lamb
　　Who died but lives again,
No more the Father's bosom shall He leave.
　His glory we proclaim,
　　His kingdom shall increase,
　O magnify His name,
　　He is the Prince of peace :
And worthy, ever worthy to receive

　　" All power,
For He shall reign and homage gain :
　　All riches,
For He bestows on friends and foes ;
　　All wisdom,
For His just mind shall judge mankind ;
　　All strength,
For His good will He shall fulfil ;
　　All honour,
For in His sight God hath delight ;
　　All glory,
For He doth shine in truth Divine ;
　　All blessing,
For as He gives all being lives ;
　　Alleluiah !

" Why do the heathen rage,
　　Imagine a vain thing,
　And earthly kings engage,
　　And rulers counsel bring
Against the Lord and His Anointed too ?

D

Why would they break their bands
    And cast away their cords?
Weak are their wilful hands,
    And weaker still their words,
For all they plot and plan, they fail to do.

"The Lord of Hosts shall laugh
    And hold them in derision,
He speaks to them in wrath
    And flings them in collision,
Yet hath He set a King on Zion's hill,
    Who all His foes shall break
        As with an iron rod;
    Be wise O kings, and make
        Submission unto God,
And learn ere 'tis too late to do His will.

"O kiss the royal Son
    And heartfelt homage pay;
If His love be not won
    Ye perish from the way,
O kiss the Son while yet His grace is free.
    But blessed are they all
        Who put their trust in Him,
    Though earthly kingdoms fall
        And mortal sight grow dim
His warm embrace new life and health will be.

"The marriage day is come,
    The Jubilee of heaven,
Of God's great wealth the sum
    Unto the Lamb is given,
Behold the crown upon His holy brow.
    He takes His royal bride,
        Adorned in robes of grace,

And seats her by His side,
  In her long promised place,
And with His own vast wealth He doth endow.

"The church of His true love
  Though oft despised by men,
Yet ever raised above
  The reach of scorn again,
Her heritage is in the Bridegroom's breast;
  His love, His life, His throne
  The faithful Church doth share,
  And heaven's polished stone
  Of whiteness shall she wear,
With her new name therein, 'My Lord's my rest.'

"Yea heaven and earth anew
  Are fashioned by His hand,
And in His sovereign view
  Spreads out a fairer land
Than any Eden seen in earth or heaven.
  Whate'er hath been before
  This work surpasseth all,
  His presence evermore
  Doth into being call
Yet fuller joys, to saints and seraphs given.

"Alleluiah!
  Blessing,
  And honour,
  And glory,
  And power,
Be unto Him that sits enthroned,
  Whose kingdom ceaseth never!
And to the Lamb who hath atoned,
  For ever and for ever!"

Again the elders fall
  In beautiful array,
Before the Lord of all,
  And as they worship, say
    "Amen!
    Alleluiah!"
The throne utters its voice,
  "Let all unite to praise
And in our God rejoice,
  Both small and great now raise
One deep response of universal joy.
For the Lord God omnipotent doth reign,
His everlasting sceptre shall maintain;
He is the Lord of lords, and King of kings,
His royal word hath made and rules all things."

Though joyful be the song
  Which swells in melody
From all the white-robed throng,
  The holy ecstacy
Of heaven flows from a deeper fountain still.
  If harmony alone
Of lip and hand were here,
  The pleasures of God's throne
Were little more we fear
Than finer treats of earthly art and skill.

Heaven drinks at Jacob's well
  Where living fountains rise,
And springs of sweetness tell
  How fertile Eden lies
Round the great well of life which ne'er is dry.
  Here is the harper's skill,
  Here the redeeming song,

Here is the source to fill
　　The bliss of all the throng,
They draw from Jacob's well and find supply.

The pure Eternal mind
　　Which in its wondrous thought,
Creation's works designed,
　　And man's perfection wrought,
Assigned the province of the human brain ;
　　And from its own deep fount
　　　Kindled the mental fires
Which in our being mount,
　　That man to God aspires,
And by His grace an empire doth obtain.

In fellowship sublime,
　　Finite with infinite,
The pilgrimage of time
　　Hath found its goal in sight
Of supreme Deity's approving face.
　　God with His saints communes,
　　　And speaks their birthright part
Not in the minstrel tunes
　　Alone, but in the heart
Of Heaven, and in His eternal grace.

The life of the unseen,
　　Is not a splendid court,
Where fashions intervene,
　　And dignities resort,
And ceremonies all affections bind :
　　No presentation day,
　　　To kiss the Monarch's hand,
One look and then away,
　　To dream how great and grand
The sov'reign's state : 'Tis nothing of the kind.

O how men covet this,
　　The royal cup to sip,
　And call it real bliss,
　　To wet their parched lip
At the same stream where earthly princes drink:
　They round the fountain press
　　Impatient for their turn,
　And though they get much less
　　Than they had hoped to earn,
'Tis something e'en to be upon the brink.

　The royal goblet's small,
　　And large the monarch's share,
　And if enough for all
　　Be not provided there,
Beneath its blight the heart begins to sore,
　And jealousies to brood,
　　And disappointments fret,
　The goblet to have viewed
　　And touched and sipped, and yet
The palate is more parched than 'twas before.

　Alas! such is all joy
　　Which comes from earth alone,
　Like the deep-veined alloy
　　That mars the precious stone:
'Tis vain and never satisfies at best.
　Or as the miser's gold,
　　It tempts men more and more,
　They like it in their hold,
　　And still increase their store,
Their greed, their selfishness, and their unrest.

　While earthly prospects wither,
　　And earthly fountains dry,

O brethren come hither,
   Let meditation fly
On wings of faith, and roam this unseen shore.
  How blest to turn aside
   Into the realms of peace ;
If earthly joys have died,
   Here heavenly ones increase
In their sweet fulness, and for evermore.

  Do we not daily pray
   Father which art in heaven ?
  Forgetting what we say
   His grace may not be given ;
He list'neth to the heart's simplicity.
  But when we humbly come
   In a true childlike trust,
  God's presence then is home ;
   We find His promise just,
And His love our supreme felicity.

  God hath a Father's heart,
   He doth not in mere name
  Profess a father's part,
   His heart feels just the same
As mine, and thine if thou art parent too.
  Yea His paternal ties
   Make ours look only small,
  In His deep heart there lies
   A love surpassing all ;
He loves as even mothers ne'er can do.

  Yet herein we delight,
   Of all the symbols shown,
  The fairest in His sight
   To make His mercy known
Was found in our parental love alone.

Like as a father cares,
   Like as a mother tends,
So our great Father wears
   Our dearest names, and blends
Father's and mother's heart into His own.

Doth not love's tender grace
   Make home what home should be?
So that we find no place
   In all the lands we see,
Where such a pure and holy fountain flows.
   This is the only leaven,
      Which makes our homes a type
   Of what we seek in heaven,
      Where every joy is ripe
In the paternal love that God bestows.

Perhaps we rarely pause
   In the hard run of life,
To ponder the pure laws
   Which rule our toil and strife,
But the grand law of home we ever feel.
   Insensibly it holds
      Our spirits near the shrine
   Of virtue, and it moulds
      Them for the home Divine,
Of which a glimpse at least it doth reveal.

O blessed home of earth,
   How often hath our breast
Been filled with childlike mirth,
   And found refreshing rest
In the sweet refuge of thy constant love?
   So surely dost thou hive
      Pure honey in thy strength,

THE UNSEEN.

That withered hearts revive,
    And venture forth at length
To battle for the better home above.

Do we e'er feel afraid
    To knock at our own door?
Or after death's dark shade
    We gain the unseen shore
Shall we approach our Father's house with fear?
    O no, where'er we roam,
        Or what our anxious care,
    We always turn to home,
        Sure of a welcome there,
We cannot doubt that heaven is less sincere.

Pity the stricken heart
    Which desolate and lone,
Hath none to heal its smart,
    By sad bereavement thrown
Into a homeless solitude of grief.
    The busy hum of life
        Unceasing all around,
    But heedless of the strife
        The homeless heart hath found,
Nor pausing to administer relief.

O let him taste the balm
    Of sympathy and love,
And point him to the calm
    Abiding home above,
Say as our Saviour did—Do not despair,
    Let not thy heart sink down,
        Or count thy troubles more,
    Than they who wear the crown
        Have undergone before,
In Jesus seek thy rest; thou'lt find it there.

Bereaved have sorrowed o'er
 The death of valued friends,
As if they must deplore
 The message Jesus sends,
To bid His faithful servants come up higher;
 Oft, too, the troubled thought
 Hath much perplexed the heart,
 Whether the Christian ought
 To cherish friends as part
Of the good hope God's promises inspire.

As if when we unloosed
 Our bark of love from earth,
A tempest was produced
 Which shattered all our mirth,
Constraining us to fling o'erboard the cheer
 Of our great Captain's grace,
 And lighten ship to sail
 Where mortal currents race,
 And human prospects pale
In the absorbing sense that heaven is near.

Nay heaven-bound saints arrive
 Not as dismantled wrecks,
Which scarce the gale survive,
 Their bare and storm-swept decks
Showing hard passage of the mortal sea;
 Not thus the Pilot brings
 His vessels into port,
 Or thus the King of kings
 Calls His beloved to court,
Putting high cost on all their dignity.

Do e'en the lost espy
 Poor Lazarus above,

And in the distant sky
 Of ever beaming love,
Behold a beggar bosomed with a saint?
 O is their vision keen
 To trace heaven's shining ranks,
Although there lies between,
 The gulf whose bridgeless banks
Fling back the echo of their fearful plaint?

So surely shall the ties
 Which death would rive in twain,
In these immortal skies
 By Christ be bound again,
Of the old earthly love no spark is lost;
 It burns as strong and true
 In this congenial clime,
As it had used to do
 When kindled first in time,
A heartfelt joy, but felt in heaven most.

Not as mere kith and kin
 Do friends in heaven unite,
But all embraced within
 Bonds of supreme delight;
All kinship hallowed by a love so pure,
 That not a thought can give
 Embarrassment or pain,
The dearest friendships live,
 And in their life obtain
Eternity to increase and endure.

O hath the mother's heart
 Offered her child to heaven,
And was it hard to part
 Though in submission given?
The child's place cooled not in the mother's breast;

THE UNSEEN.

Still warm e'en after death
  Her offspring to embrace,
  The loss of mortal breath
  Dimmed not the mother's face,
Christ read her looks of love and gave her rest.

Death may the body kill,
  But cannot hurt the soul,
  He makes the heart stand still,
  But then hath spent the whole
Of his great power; and while he claims the right
  To bury in the grave
  The spoils of mortal strife,
  All heaven bends to save
  The precious blood-bought life
Which springs uninjured from the fearful fight.

True many mansions here
  Uplift their towers on high,
  And palaces appear
  All radiant as the sky,
Yet every mansion hath an open door;
  And every portal shines
  With welcome from within,
  And every heart inclines
  Unto its sacred kin,
To interchange affection more and more.

Here is a wealth untold,
  A wealth exceeding all
  The silver and the gold,
  That mortals riches call;
Here are distinctions, but distinctions blend
  In one deep central heart,
  Which in its hate of pride,

Giveth the humblest part
    With princes side by side,
And every beaming face proclaims a friend.

No selfishness is here,
    It thriveth but in hell;
Not in this holy sphere,
    Such evil tempers dwell;
But love from the great Father's fountain-breast
  Strikes its Divine roots down,
    And spreads them forth, until
  The hosts beneath His crown
    Move only by His will,
And drinking at His heart find filial rest.

Love, Paradise sustains,
    Or heaven itself would sink,
Love healeth all the pains,
    Love is the meat and drink,
The toil and recreation of the saints;
  Love is in their pursuits
    Adorneth Zion's bowers,
  Love ripeneth the fruits,
    Is fragrant in the flowers,
Wipes away tears, and hushes all complaints.

O blessed, blessed balm,
    Distilled beneath the throne,
Proceeding in a calm
    Deep flood from God alone;
It floweth nearer! yea it flows to me!
  In this stream let me dip
    My robes, and make them pure,
  These waters let me sip,
    Yea drink, and thus ensure
A heavenly grace, meet, Lord, to be with Thee.

Of all Thy saints, the least
  In such a home as this,
Enjoys a royal feast
  Of everlasting bliss ;
But it is " Home, sweet home," which is so dear.
  The love, the warmth, the feel
    That neither care nor foe
  Can e'er disturb its weal,
    As in the home below,
The sense of oneness and the Father near.

No separations part
  The family of heaven,
No changes blight the heart
  With saddening leaven,
The Father never fears that " one is not ; "
  For each child is a part
    Of His infinite soul,
  And in His mighty heart
    He doth embrace the whole,
And by His own life guarantees their lot.

The Heavenly Vine extends
  Its branches far and wide,
With luscious fruit it bends,
  Though once it drooped and died ;
But by its death gives immortality
  To tender branches graft,
    Which, pruned with patient care,
  Outgrow the spoiler's craft,
    And richer produce bear,
To swell the vintage of eternity.

But above all, the thought
  Most precious here is this,

That He whose grace hath bought
    Such heritage of bliss,
Is in Himself its true eternal joy.
    The heavenward way hath beamed
        From Jesu's blood-stained breast,
    The family redeemed
        Find everlasting rest
In Him, and for Him all their powers employ.

    Christ o'er His people reigns,
        To Him they lowly bend,
    But He in mercy deigns
        To call them each His friend,
To own their kinship and embrace them all ;
    Not as a King apart,
        Displays His royal grace,
    But with them heart to heart
        And mingling face to face,
Has kindly words of love for great and small.

    To feel the loving hand
        Of Jesus in their own,
    And traverse all the land
        That spreads around the throne,
Where living fountains of delight arise ;
    To hear His friendly voice
        The Father's will expound,
    Makes every heart rejoice,
        And happiness abound,
And heaven more and more a Paradise.

    Not one of all the vast
        Array of mansions here,
    From first unto the last
        But Jesus oft is there,
Within the range of His omniscient view,

There is no hallowed spot,
   No sphere of heavenly rest,
No recompense or lot,
   But He prepared and blest,
O hath my Lord prepared a place for you?

He is no stranger where
   Each threshold knows His foot,
His sonship He doth share,
   And all His glory put
So freely in the presence of His own ;
   That they are blent with Him,
     In His true likeness shine,
   No garment soiled or dim,
     But every robe Divine,
Fit in its warp and weft to grace a throne.

O Jesus is so near
   So intimate and free,
His converse doth endear
   His heaven-born family,
In each celestial house He sitteth down ;
   As though He were again
     At Bethany of old,
   But not as there in pain,
     Death's havoc to behold,
Yet with a tender heart beneath His crown.

The uncreated Sun
   Drives every cloud away,
And life is now begun
   In bright eternal day :
Truly the light is sweet, for many shades
   Made earthly vision dim,
     God's dispensations dull,

That Christian joy in Him
  Was rarely at the full,
But here it lives, and never, never fades.

  He sheds upon the mind
    A clear, immortal light,
  He breaks the seals that bind
    The range of mortal sight,
And bids it penetrate the deep profound
  Of mysteries, unseen,
    Save Deity alone,
  Because the veil between,
    Suspended from the throne,
Hid in its awful folds the holy ground.

  The providential scrolls
    Which in His archives lie,
  He graciously unrolls
    Before His people's eye,
Revealing secrets of their history.
  As with a key of gold
    He openeth the mind,
  Its native powers unfold,
    And in their new birth find,
A wondrous kinship to infinity.

  The trials and the tears
    Which they endured on earth,
  Starting so many fears
    Of unbelieving birth,
He shows them woven in His sacred loom
  So wisely and so well
    That they admire them now;
  Though once 'twas hard to tell,
    When anguish wrung the brow,
Were they the children's good, or children's doom?

The deeply heart-dyed thread
   Inlaid with chafing pain,
When the affections bled
   And left their crimson stain,
Is now most beautiful in all the robe ;
   It with a pureness shines
     Which angels love to see,
   And as they trace its lines,
     They solve the mystery
Of suffering, and the great Healer's probe.

Though rough the path they trod,
   It was the King's highway,
The sympathy of God
   Watched every step that lay
On life's hard road, for He had paced it too
   With bruised and bleeding feet,
     And tempted as we are ;
   O how His heart doth beat
     For pilgrims still afar,
And min'st'ring spirits sends to bear them through.

The hot refining fire
   A purer grace supplied,
As it burned higher and higher,
   The faith thus keenly tried
Lost all its dross, and sevenfold value gained.
   Behold it glitter now
     Clear as a brilliant star,
   Upon the sacred brow
     Which once the thorns did scar,
And drops of mortal anguish deeply stained.

The sufferings of time
   By stricken saints endured,

Here shed a light sublime
　　　　On things which they obscured;
　　And God's Almighty love is mirrored most
　　　In trials that they thought
　　　　Were hard for them to bear,
　　And precious gems were wrought
　　　In sorrow, which they wear
In crowns of joy, and of which crowns may boast.

　　　The dignity of man
　　　　Lay in his own free will,
　　Though oft athwart the plan
　　　God taught him to fulfil,
Yet Godlike in his liberty was made;
　　　A liberty abused
　　　　To follow evil ways,
　　And daringly refused
　　　To render God the praise
His righteousness demanded should be paid.

　　　He would not be a King
　　　　O'er men whom He constrained
　　Allegiance to bring;
　　　If thus Jehovah reigned,
The glory of His kingdom would be gone,
　　　Its lustre sullied down
　　　　By such a rule of fate;
　　'Twould blemish e'en His crown,
　　　If men must love and hate,
By law which granted liberty to none.

　　　If in His royal grace
　　　　The King would not allow
　　Man's moral freedom place,
　　　But made His servants bow
Without capacity to disobey:

E 2

Could that be moral law,
  Or honour in such rule?
Nay, Deity must abhor
  To fashion man a fool,
And rather not create than own such sway.

No doubt He well foreknew
  That such high moral good
Would involve evil too,
  And that the precious blood
Of His own Son for sinners must be shed;
  Yet choosing not to stint
    The bounty of His plan,
  His own hand did imprint
    The penalty of man
On Christ, who bore it to the cross and bled.

Thus suffering was made
  A pruning knife of keen
And well-attempered blade,
  That it hath ever been
The husbandman's best means to train the vine.
  Hence all before the throne
    Have felt its bitter smart,
  But sympathy was shown
    By Jesu's tender heart,
For He hath trod the press and gives the wine.

"My saints with me have died,"
  He cries, "but now ye live,
Ye shall be glorified
  With me, and I will give
Right to the banquet of my Father's grace.
  With me ye suffered, and
    With me ye all shall reign,

THE UNSEEN.

Henceforth ye take your stand
  The foremost of my train,
And at my banquet fill a royal place.

" In battle we have fought,
    And felt one common pain,
  In labour we have wrought
    To build God's house again,
Which sin had ruined, though a house Divine.
  One kin, one grief, one strife,
    One wrestling with the foe,
  One death, one grave, one life
    Doth bind us, and ye know
The bond omnipotent is mine and thine.

" No foe the tie shall rend,
    Unless he rend my heart,
  Our heritage doth blend
    In one eternal part,
And whoso spoileth you must first destroy
  My everlasting strength;
    My sceptre break,
  Yea, traverse the whole length
    Of heaven, and o'ertake
Eternity, ere he can bar your joy."

O what a wealth of mind
    In these high courts is found,
  To fellowship inclined,
    Open to all, unbound;
Not as in finite spheres of gifted men,
  Where thought too oft is stored
    In realms so few can gain,
  That feeble wings have soared,
    But fluttered down in pain,
With hardly courage left to try again.

The hindrances which cramp
    Mind in its earthly mould,
And fix their brazen stamp
    On rich and well-wrought gold.
Have no allowance in this holy sphere.
  No bigotry survives,
    Although by no means rare,
  In heaven it never thrives
    For lack of native air,
However rank on earth, it grows not here.

  So sadly hath it spoiled
    A mind of noble thought,
  So deeply hath it soiled
    The beauty God hath wrought,
That heaven disowns it with instinct disdain.
  'Tis plucked up by the roots
    Like as an evil weed;
  So perish all its fruits,
    Nor ever shall its seed
In Eden find a soil to life regain.

  How truly great and grand
    The intellect of man,
  The touch of God's right hand
    Gives it a strength to span
With firmest tread where oft it slipped before;
  To burst the narrow ties
    Which held in leading strings;
  And fills with sweet surprise
    That here eternal things
Can be defamed by bigotry no more.

  On every glowing brow
    The Lamb imprints His seal,

His Father's name is now
   Sufficient to reveal
The Church to which His followers belong.
  Nor is their saintship scared
   To see so near the throne,
  Brethren they never dared
   While yet on earth to own ;
But heaven puts right all that the earth had wrong.

  The Father's name is Love,
   And written on a scale
  That every saint above
   Is held within its pale,
High church, or Low, or ought the sect he bore.
  Heaven's charity is wide,
   And like the great deep sea
  Receives in its flood tide
   All streams, nor can there be
An ebb, to bare what love hath covered o'er.

  'Tis true that no dissent
   Doth vex the peace of heaven,
  But high church zeal intent
   On purging out such leaven
As a defilement of the Bread of Life ;
  Will find e'en heaven bare,
   If it would only feed
  On apostolic fare,
   And its succession seed :
Heaven will not starve on apostolic strife.

  Though 'tis a dainty meat,
   Luxuriously shared
  By those that cannot eat
   Of what their Lord prepared,
So curious alas is their depression,

That they begin to waste
    The wholesome food of truth,
  And so to suit their taste
    The tempter's skill forsooth
Must dress them " Apostolical succession."

But at the heavenly feast,
    Where countless thousands sup,
  The greatest and the least
    Hand round the friendly cup
Which bears the royal arms of Charity ;
  And as they freely drink
    All truly have one heart,
  And wonderingly they think
    How strangely earth did part
Them once with notions of disparity.

A brotherhood at length
    Of real Godlike men,
  Grand in their moral strength,
    Not as in ages when
They could not o'er the gospel rules agree :
  Though so Divinely taught,
    Yet failing oft to see
  That man's immortal thought
    Was not, and ne'er could be
Kneaded like infants learning A, B, C.

The empire of the mind
    Is varied in its view ;
  Heaven will never bind,
    As bigots fain would do,
Man's noble intellect to flutter o'er
  The ground with little grace ;
    Nay, God doth give him wing

THE UNSEEN.

To sweep the realms of space,
   Not like the crippled thing
Which bigots would send limping through
    heaven's door.

Here is in mind a grip,
   A conscious power to deal
With things which earth let slip,
   As under lock and seal.
Nor doth the reverence of heav'n disdain
   To take an infant's hand,
    And teach it to explore
   The glories of the land,
    Or cull from Eden's store
A richer dower than earthly sages gain.

The feeblest mental eye
   Is focussed in a light,
Which helps it to descry
   Worlds passing mortal sight,
Or glimmered but in telescopes below.
   Great realms of life are near
    Which earth has never known,
   To heaven's vision clear,
    Mere suburbs of the throne,
With min'st'ring spirits passing to and fro.

Bright worlds distinctly seen
   Shine forth in beauty rare,
Where sin hath never been
   To spoil God's creatures there,
They had their trial but they stood the test;
   Retained primeval grace,
    No gift of heaven lost,
   And in the Father's face,
    They live without the cost
Which bought our heavenly heritage and rest.

No sin, or fear, or shame,
  No disobedient fall,
No suffering or pain,
  No death to spread its pall,
No graves to dig, no epitaphs to write,
  No homes rent into gaps,
    No loved ones dead and gone,
  No separation saps
    The hopes they build upon,
No cloud to dim their everlasting light.

They hold their birthright still,
  As rich as it was given,
And hence Jehovah's will
  Hath made their birthright heaven,
But holiness knits all in kindred bonds.
  They never knew our loss,
    They never felt our fears,
  Nor ever at the cross
    Shed penitential tears,
Yet to our filial joy their joy responds.

United in the same
  Inheritance of grace,
In which through Jesu's name
  We hold a pardoned place;
Forgiven now they love us, and they yearn
  To hear how 'twas we fell,
    How Mercy raised us up,
  And shut the gate of hell,
    So that salvation's cup
No subtle tempter should again o'erturn.

Heaven's godliness is true,
  Its sympathy in play,

And it has work to do,
 Nor tires through all the day
Which never darkens with the setting sun ;
 The example of its God
  Marks all its duties down,
 And earnest paths are trod
  In rev'rence to the crown ;
His will is active, and His will is done.

 O God forbid that I,
  Foster a foolish thought,
 But to my mental eye
  Vast worlds which Thou hast wrought,
Thronged with intelligence spread far and near.
 Our native earth but seems
  An atom in Thy sight,
 And space unmeasured teems
  With realms of life and light,
Creations of Thy power and love appear.

 Thy royalty demands
  With a right kingly will,
 And Thy almighty hands
  Are equal to fulfil
All Thy benevolence and grace design.
 O is it not Thy voice
  Still crying "Let there be?"
 Do not new worlds rejoice
  In Thy great sovereignty,
And witness to their origin Divine?

 Didst Thou in six days spend
  Thy everlasting strength?
 Six days bring to an end
  Thy works, and all the length
Of Thy eternity run into seven?

Six days could ne'er despoil
 So deep and rich a mine;
Nor days' or ages' toil
 To passive rest incline
The industry which founded earth and heaven.

Doth not life flow from Thee
 Which knows no count of days,
The living yet to be
 Heard in eternal praise
Of unexhausted Majesty Divine?
 Doth not the fountain spring,
 And do not streamlets flow,
That worlds on worlds may bring
 The harvest which we know
Must ripen where Thy royal face doth shine?

The paradise of rest
 Is not for idle men,
Who think the saints are blest
 With service now and then,
But in their leisure most, with nought to do:
 All easy on the wing,
 Or bowered in repose,
Or it may be, a sing,
 That mortal wants and woes
Have passed for ever from their troubled view.

Could earnest souls desire
 A paradise like this?
Or such a hope inspire
 The men whose real bliss
Has been to honour Christ and ne'er deny;
 Who spend their latest breath
 Rejoicing with their Lord,

That both in life and death
 They have fulfilled the word
Of Him whose presence welcomes them on high?
 Nay, if there be at ease
  In Zion's courts on earth
 Those that themselves would please,
  And care not for the dearth
Which their own selfishness hath spread around;
 Whose best idea of heaven
  Is just to fill their breast
 With such high-sweetened leaven,
  That they may ever rest ;
Not in the Father's house will such be found.

 O let us rather grasp
  The precious living seed,
 With sickle in our clasp,
  And ripe in faith and deed,
Yea bowed with sheaves may we in heaven appear ;
 All harnessed for fresh toil
  With God's eternal Son,
 And strong to bear new spoil
  To Him, whose kind " Well done ! "
Makes every labour rest and duty dear.

 Jesus I fain would stand
  In presence of Thy throne,
 Still cleaving in my hand
  The sword which hath o'erthrown
Thy enemies and mine: with beaten shield,
 And stains of earnest fight ;
  Than bring an unscarred face
 Into my Captain's sight,
  On which He cannot trace
A soldier's service in the battle-field.

O God as we draw nigher,
  We feel Thy presence burn
With an intenser fire,
  And glow with grand concern
Of plans benevolent ; a motive power
Proceeding from Thy throne,
  Which moves the life of all,
And bidding every drone
  With talents great or small,
Shake off his sloth, and waste no precious hour.

O what a mighty force
  In heavenly energy,
The central ruling source
  Of all activity ;
Keeping its inner life so fresh and pure,
Eternity flows on,
  But not a mark of age
Allowed to rest upon
  The infant or the sage ;
Their powers increase, their energies endure.

Ten thousand ages past,
  Or twice ten thousand more,
All reckoning at last
  Must surely give it o'er,
Heav'n's earnest face still fronts eternity;
Developing its mind
  And widening its range,
So clear and unconfined,
  That perfect pleasures change
In endless glories of infinity.

Heaven's hosts are on the wing
  Full of Divine intent,

THE UNSEEN.

The bounty of the King
    Is generously spent,
That saints and angels are like flames of fire;
    Burning with hallowed zeal
        To bear the royal grace,
    And longing to reveal
        The pleasure of His face,
They minister His will, and never tire.

O heaven! thou'rt richer far
    Than these weak thoughts have told;
There shineth not a star,
    There glittereth not in gold,
There flasheth not in jewelry of kings;
    There speaketh not a tongue,
        There painteth not in art,
    There singeth not in song,
        Conceiveth not a heart
To represent the half of heavenly things.

Yet heaven must begin
    Where beats the human heart,
The kingdom is within;
    O Jesus! grant me part,
And by Thy cross help me to hold my crown:
    O may Thy grace increase
        The hope already given,
    Till ripened in the peace
        And perfect bliss of heav'n,
I see Thy face, and by Thy side sit down.

SONGS IN TRIAL.

THE DISABLED LABOURER'S DREAM.

>Full in my sight,
>The fields were white,
>Already in harvest-tide,
>The sun was high
>In Autumn sky,
>As reapers their sickles plied.

>The Master's voice
>Made all rejoice,
>As He cheered His willing men;
>The sickles bright
>Glanced in the light
>As the stroke swept round again.

>The busy throng,
>With cheerful song,
>Toiled on in the broiling sun;
>But at the gates
>A labourer waits,
>As if the day's work were done.

>His head was bent,
>His look intent,
>On the busy reapers all:

His eye was sad,
I thought he had
A fresh tear ready to fall.

Upon his breast
His weak arm press'd,
It strengthless and helpless lay;
And then I thought
That arm had wrought
On many a harvest day.

A tear it cost,
That he had lost
The strength of active workers.
It might have been
That he had seen
The harvest wait for reapers.

The tear was dry,
And bright his eye,
As the work was surely done;
"Though I'm not there,
Lord, hear my prayer
For the toilers in the sun."

And as he knelt,
A thrill he felt
Of strength came with the prayer.
Perhaps, ere long,
He may wax strong,
And reap with the workers there.

" Lord, strong or weak,
Thy will I seek,
I adore Thy will alone.

> Lord, I believe
> I shall receive
> My due in the Harvest Home."

MATLOCK.
July 17th, 1872.

MY CROSS.

Oft it was a cross to me,
Lord, to speak the truth for Thee;
But the cross is greater now,
That I must in silence bow
To the teaching of Thy will,
While I hear Thy voice, " Be still."

The cross Thou bidd'st me to bear,
Thy love hath promised to share,
Though it be heavy to me,
'Twill lighten when cast on Thee;
I fail, if in self I try,
I gain, if self I deny.

SOUTHPORT, 1872.

THE CHILD'S PRAYER AND THE FATHER'S ANSWER.

Composed to the music, in "AMERICAN SONGSTER," *of* "Father, take my hand."

The storm is fierce, my Father; the waves roll
Deep and high, and the swell alarms my soul.

The winds beat roughly down and overwhelm
My feeble bark. O, Father! take the helm,
  And through the storm my Pilot be,
    Pilot be, Pilot be,
Pilot Thy trembling child.

Fear not, I am thy Father. I will save
My anxious child from the treacherous wave.
The storm beats o'er thee, but it shall not harm,
And thou shalt surely prove how sweet the calm.
  Hear now thy Father's voice, "Be still,"
    "Peace, be still; peace, be still;
Thy fears be still, my child."

The conflict's close, my Father, and the foe
Presses his great strength hard to lay me low;
He lifts his giant head and proudly boasts
Defiance against Thee, O Lord of Hosts.
  If thus to Thee, what then to me,
    Then to me, then to me,
Thy weak and helpless child?

Be strong and trust thy Father. In the fight
I will shed on thee heaven's holy light,
And the great cloud of witnesses shall see
How thou canst battle and o'ercome for Me.
  Take now thy shield, and quench his darts,
    Fi'ry darts, fi'ry darts,
Quench all his darts, My child.

My ties are breaking, Father, and my heart
Is well nigh broken too, as friends depart
And leave me in my sorrow all alone;
Fain would I be with them before Thy throne,
  And gladly join to worship Thee,
    Only Thee, only Thee,
No more alone Thy child.

Alone! and with thy Father! I will fill
Thy heart with sweetest company, until
Thy tears are dried, and thy earth-broken ties
Are golden bonds to link thee to the skies.
   My sacred oath, I will not leave,
      Never leave, never leave
   My lone yet loving child.

Heaven is my home, Father. For its sake
And for Thine I now patiently partake
Of pain and loss. I bend my will to Thine
For heaven and all in heaven are mine.
   I am joint-heir with Christ the King,
      Christ the King, Christ the King,
   With Christ shall reign Thy child.

My child thou'rt near thy Father, and thy home
Is not far from thee while thou still dost roam
On earth. The path is short which lies between
The temporal and the eternal scene.
   Thy Father's hand will lift the veil,
      Lift the veil, lift the veil,
   And God will crown His child.

HOYLAKE,
   November, 1872.

SUNSET AT SEA.

I PACED worn rocks and in the west
The sun sank grandly to his rest,
In robes of honour richly drest,
   Crimson, silver, and gold;

Right royal King in monarch's state,
Bright clouds as humble courtiers wait,
In willing homage round the great ;
　　Wondering, I behold !

While gazing on the sunset scene,
A low'ring cloud was roll'd between,
As full of envy it had been,
　　I shivered in its shade.
Yet cheerful beams burst through and through,
And cast their radiance in view,
Beyond the dark'ning cloud which threw
　　A frown to make it fade.

The gloomy cloud they did infold,
Burnished its sullen edge with gold,
Till by deep contrast as it rolled,
　　Illumed by light behind,
The sun appeared to shine yet more
Brightly than he had done before,
And as I lingered on the shore
　　I pondered in my mind.

I mused on moral clouds, and felt
That darkest shades could weave no belt
To bind the light which God hath dealt
　　To the believing soul.
Temptation's edge the light will gild,
Trial with blessing shall be filled,
And heav'n-born grace shall be instilled
　　To harmonise the whole.

Darkness intensifies the light,
And shadows blend with sunbeams bright,
Contrasts are pleasant to the sight,
　　And fondly gazed upon.

So faith in trial doth outshine
All radiant with light Divine,
O may this precious faith be mine,
  Through God's eternal Son.

HOYLAKE,
  November, 1872.

LISTEN TO ME.

LISTEN to me, my Father, while I pray,
Turn not Thy holy loving heart away,
Incline Thine ear while I bow down to Thee;
In tender mercy,—O listen to me.

Listen to me;—for in Thy yoke I serve,
The yoke make easy, and my soul preserve
In sacred peace and true humility;
Thus would I learn;—O Lord, listen to me.

Listen to me:—beneath the cross I bend,
Lest it too heavy prove, Thy succour send
To hold my spirit up, and keep it free
From sinful murm'ring;—O listen to me.

Listen to me:—if in Thy holy love
The bitter cup may possibly remove;
If to Thy servant thus it cannot be,
Help me to drink it;—Lord, listen to me.

Listen to me, while I walk through the vale,
Which is so near to death that mortals quail,
Because they see its shadow, yet with Thee
No evil will I fear;—O listen to me.

Listen to me :—I'm but a pilgrim here,
And to my Father's house am getting near;
O save me from all sin that I may see
My Saviour's glory ;—Lord, listen to me.

HOYLAKE,
   November, 1872.

ACTIVE AND PASSIVE DUTY.

Dark thoughts had thrown
A midnight gloom
Upon the path I trod ;
And fierce despair
Was seeking where
To tempt my heart from God.

My faith was tried,
And feebly cried
How long ! O Lord, how long ?
So faint my hope,
I blindly grope,
And nearly hushed my song.

Why am I here
While work is there,
And labourers are few ?
Why doth Thy will
Command " Be still,"
Why not command " To do ? "

   * * * * * *   *

Hark ! The alarm
Disturbs the calm
Of the still village round :

SONGS IN TRIAL.

    The life-boat's call
    To seamen all,
And well they know the sound.

    The gun! The gun!
    In haste we run
To the sea-beach hard by,
    And on the wave
    Gallant and brave,
The life-boat we descry.

    The night is dark,
    A tiny spark
Of starlight here and there.
" Bend to the oar,
    The ship's ashore
On the sunk rocks! Beware!"

    For boat and men,
    Again, again,
Give a right hearty cheer,
    Both long and loud
    From all the crowd,
Till the wrecked sailors hear.

    Who does not crave
    To reach and save
You weather-beaten crew?
    Who does not pray,
    Lord speed the way
Of the brave men to you?

    Ah! this I thought
    Is what I ought
To do as work for God:

Pull through the wave,
And lost ones save
From sin's deceitful flood.

✧　✧　✧　✧　✧　✧　✧　✧

But look ashore,
How more and more
The light-house sheds its beam:
Quiet it stands
On lonely lands,
Yet lights the tidal stream.

Both wreck and boat
And all afloat,
On active duty bound,
Have for a guide
Upon the tide
The light it shines around.

In darkened night,
Amid the fight
Of waves, the watch looked out:
"Thank God" his prayer,
"The light is there,
Put the ship's helm about."

The dreadful fear,
Which made him steer
In anxious doubt, was gone,
He blessed the beam
Which he had seen,
His ship went safely on.

Now Lord I see,
That I may be
Silent yet full of light;

A beam to shine
From time to time
On toilers in the night.

If I may not
Pull in the boat
To reach the shiv'ring wreck,
If Thou forbidd'st
Me in the midst
Of seamen on the deck,

Then be it mine,
To brightly shine
Out on the gloomy sea,
Their blessing gain
Upon the main,
And recompense from Thee,

HOYLAKE,
   November, 1872.

TRUST IN CHRIST.

Jesu, listen to my cry,
  While I lift my heart to Thee,
For Thy tender love I sigh,
  Cast Thy gracious smile on me.
I adore Thy right Divine
  To my confidence and love,
Sanctify this heart of mine,
  Lead me to the land above.

I have seen Thee on the cross,
  I have wept beneath Thy feet,

I have counted all things loss
   That I may with Jesus meet.
As the branch is in the vine,
   As it cleaveth to the tree,
Fully knit my heart to Thine,
   Lord, I would abide in Thee.

Thou art true when others fail,
   Thou art love when others hate,
Thou art nigh when foes assail,
   Thou dost rule my whole estate.
Fain I would Thy witness be
   Among those who love Thee not,
That Thine enemies may see
   Priceless treasure I have got.

Often I have vowed before
   To confess Thee unto men,
But my vows were scarcely o'er
   Ere I broke them all again.
Lord I would more watchful be,
   Taking warning from the past,
Seeking greater strength from Thee,
   Proving faithful at the last.

HOYLAKE,
   December, 1872.

THE DYING CHILD.

MOTHER tell me of my home,
   Which you say is in the sky,
Where the good delight to roam,
   And the holy angels fly.

SONGS IN TRIAL.

It will soothe my pain,
To hear you again
Speak of the rest I hope to attain.

Child it is a lovely place,
More adorned than I can tell,
Beautiful in ev'ry grace,
Where God and His people dwell,
No palace so fair
As the mansions there,
And one for thee our Lord will prepare.

Its walls are of jasper built,
Its foundations precious stone,
And the whole city is gilt
With glory from Jesu's throne:
The city is bright
With a burning light
Which never goes out in day or night.

Each gate of a pearl is made,
And beams like a silv'ry star,
Its street with fine gold is laid,
Which glitters as glass afar.
No lamp ever shone
Like that on the throne,
Burning undimmed as a crystal stone.

And Jesus Himself is there,
Exalted at God's right hand,
And the saints His conquest share,
As they all around Him stand.
An emerald bow,
In radiant glow,
The seat of the King doth brightly show.

Their robes are white as the moon,
Their crowns are bright as the sun,

SONGS IN TRIAL.

Their harps in melod'ous tune,
   And they sing of vict'ries won :
    Through trouble they came
    Confessing the name,
Bearing the sign of the bleeding Lamb.

o o o o o o o o

Mother dear, when I have seen
   All the wonders you have told,
The rainbow's emerald green,
   And the pearls and gems and gold ;
    I shall look for more
    In my Saviour's store,
As I tread that calm and peaceful shore.

Tell me what then I shall do,
   And who there will be to love;
Shall I be parted from you
   In that grand city above?
    It would pierce my heart
    Like a cruel dart
If from my loving mother I part.

I want very much to know
   What my duty there will be,
And ere to that home I go,
   Shall I my dear mother see?
    If I leave thee now,
    In heaven wilt thou
Imprint thy kiss on my beaming brow?

o o o o o o o o

My child, when in yon bright land,
   Thy mother thou wilt not need,
For Jesus will take thine hand,
   And to living fountains lead,

SONGS IN TRIAL.

Which flow from the throne
In pure streams unknown
By all who neglect their Lord to own.

Sorrow there thou canst not feel,
God shall wipe all tears from thee,
And thy youthful brow will seal
With the stamp of royalty.
The hand of the King
With His signet ring,
Shall mark thee an heir beneath His wing.

* * * * * * * *

Mother, if in heaven above
I need not thy care as now,
Happy in my Saviour's love
While before His throne I bow.
If His holy will
My affections fill,
A place there will be for mother still.

If I serve with all my heart,
More God does not ask of me;
Never will He let me part
With the love I bear to thee.
Our love is Divine,
My mother's and mine,
And love like that can never decline.

Thou hast taught me how to pray,
And to sing of yon bright band,
Thou hast led me in the way
To that holy happy land;
The land of delight,
Where there is no night
To cast its dark shadows on the sight.

I am near the city now,
   Angels fair are on the wing,
Light is shining on my brow,
   Listen!—I can hear them sing.
    So sweetly they sound
    Their harps all around,
O mother this must be heav'nly ground.

When I stand within the gate,
   Free from ev'ry stain of sin,
At the portals I shall wait
   Till my mother enter in;
    And there I will sing
    All praise to the King,
For mother to heav'n Jesus will bring.

Or my Lord may let me be
   A bright guardian-angel near,
Ministering unto thee
   Strength to aid in times of fear;
    When I hear thy cry,
    O swiftly I'll fly
To dry the tear in thy glistening eye.

   ✿   ✿   ✿   ✿   ✿   ✿   ✿   ✿

But my dear one it may be,
   That we meet not as we part,
When thou dost thy mother see,
   Heaven may absorb thine heart;
    God's child thou wilt be,
    Not a child to me,
But more than mother's His love to thee.

   ✿   ✿   ✿   ✿   ✿   ✿   ✿   ✿

Mother dearest, I am thine,
   Part of thy undying life,

And God tells me, thou art mine,
  Nor shall death's last mortal strife
    E'er sever us twain ;
    We shall meet again
Mother and child on the holy plain.

I shall know my mother's face,
  I shall feel my mother's love,
When we mutually embrace
  In our blessed home above.
    If thee I caress
    Still Jesus will bless,
He will be sure I love Him no less.

I shall see thee sitting down
  On the right hand of the throne,
And behold thee wear thy crown,
  For thou wilt not be alone.
    We all shall be there
    Thy triumph to share,
And a true welcome sweetly declare.

Hosts of angels will be near,
  Jesus will be nearer still,
If thou lookest, mother dear,
  By thy side on Zion's hill
    Thou wilt find me, too,
    As thou'rt used to do
In these days of love so tried and true.

  ✿ ✿ ✿ ✿ ✿ ✿ ✿ ✿

Death's stream ripples on my feet,
  " Jesus help Thy little one,
Jordan's swell is cold and deep,
  Blessed Lord, I come, I come!

>   I pant for Thy breast,
>   And there I would rest,
>   A lamb in Thy fold for ever blest."

❀ ❀ ❀ ❀ ❀ ❀ ❀ ❀

>   Fain the mother's longing eye
>   Now would pierce the closing veil,
>   See her darling in the sky,
>   But the earthly light is pale;
>   The curtain is drawn
>   Till the day shall dawn,
>   The night must pass ere the coming morn.
>
>   Dark'ning shadows intervene,
>   Closing round the youthful saint,
>   Dimly gazing on the scene
>   Till her mother's heart is faint,
>   Her deep stricken cry
>   Goes up through the sky,
>   And God looks down with pitying eye.
>
>   Ling'ring, weeping, sad and lone,
>   Life with keen bereavement wrung,
>   Suddenly a light is thrown
>   Through heav'n's gate wide open flung;
>   A beam full of love
>   From the throne above,
>   And hov'ring round like a gentle dove,
>
>   Sweetly on her spirit falls
>   Like dew on with'ring flowers;
>   While a voice from heaven calls
>   To the celestial bowers,
>   "Thy child is at rest
>   In the Saviour's breast,
>   Follow! and thou shalt be ever blest."

HOYLAKE,
   December, 1872.

BELLS.

Midnight bells ring merrily,
Let me listen quietly,
If inclined to listen, too,
I will tell my thoughts to you.

Precious moments fleeting go,
Precious, for I love them so,
Precious memories remain,
Precious resolutions gain.

Precious year, 'tis at an end,
We are parting with a friend;
Real friends are very few,
Shall we gain one in the new?

While I hear the merry bell,
I regret to say farewell,
But a weakness at my heart
Tells me dearest friends must part.

Let us, therefore, part in peace,
Fretful thoughts for ever cease,
Precious gifts are yet in store,
Christ is mine for evermore.

Precious year, though well begun,
Stained with sin ere it was done,
Precious Saviour, pardon me,
Daily make me more like Thee.

Precious vows I make anew,
Grant me grace to keep them too,
Print on me Thy seal Divine,
And preserve me ever Thine.

Precious trials in the past,—
Trials do not ever last,—

Precious lessons we may learn,
Precious heritages earn.

Precious joys have fled away,
Joys are not for ev'ry day,
While I do Thy holy will,
Precious peace abideth still.

Precious light on holy mount,
Many sunny scenes I count,
Precious rest in soothing shade,
When in lowly vale I laid.

Precious years may bud and fade,
God still sends both light and shade,
"God is light," and to the end,
Light or shade, will be my Friend.

Merry bells the new year ring,
Joys and sorrows it will bring,
On my God I cast my care,
He will bless me everywhere.

Precious faith my heart within,
Old year out and new year in :
Merry bells ring loud and long,
God shall have my grateful song.

HOYLAKE,
   December 31*st*, 1872.

"BLESS ME."

O God, my Father, hear my prayer,
And let me with Thy children share
Thy sacred gifts both rich and free,
Bless me, O Father, even me.

SONGS IN TRIAL.

If trial weigh my spirit down,
And I provoke my Father's frown,
Yet all unworthy let me see,
Thou wilt in love bless even me.

If Satan tempt me to repine,
And murmur at the will Divine,
O Lord my great Redeemer be,
And bless with vict'ry even me.

If hope deferred excite my fears,
And stain my cheek with bitter tears,
Still let my will with Thine agree,
And wait assured Thou wilt bless me.

Not as the world giveth I desire,
Of worldly gifts my heart would tire,
Speak as of old, Lord, speak to me,
"My peace thy sacred blessing be."

If my faith tremble in its hold,
Thy deeper truth to me unfold.
Faint yet pursuing after Thee,
I feel Thou dost bless even me.

HOYLAKE,
December, 1872.

DEVOTION.

JESUS, what may I do for Thee
How can I best Thy witness be?
Fill my whole soul with light Divine,
In all my daily life outshine.

Incline me now Thy touch to feel,
Press deeply in my heart Thy seal,

Dwell in me as Thy pure abode,
And wrap me in Thy royal robe.

A living temple I would be,
With all my powers worship Thee,
Filled with the incense of Thy love,
And fragrant as the courts above.

Breathe in my heart the quenchless fire,
My soul with living faith inspire,
Faith which shall pierce the veil between,
And gaze into the things unseen.

Shall I on Thy great Throne sit down?
Am I Thine heir to wear a crown?
O may its lustre even now,
Shine in true glory on my brow.

HOYLAKE,
   January, 1873.

DEVOTION.

O GOD! with Thee I humbly plead
For grace to help in time of need,
Let mercy now Thy succour bear,
And bless me while I bend in prayer.

Revive the life of grace within,
Cleanse me from all the seeds of sin,
Let nothing root or bud in me,
But what is planted, Lord, by Thee.

Help me to daily bear the cross,
No matter what my worldly loss,
From Thee I shall have richer gain,
And with Thee shall for ever reign.

I follow Thee, and self deny,
For Jesus I would live and die,
Let me Thy holy strength partake,
And witness for my Master's sake.

O let me closely cleave to Thee,
That the dull world may truly see,
How Christ doth fill the human soul,
How grace doth sanctify the whole.

HOYLAKE,
   January, 1873.

COVENANT.

O God! wilt Thou regard my cry,
While humbly at Thy feet I lie?
Awed by the light of Thy pure throne
I mourn my sins to Thee alone.

With heartfelt grief I ponder now
My oft-repeated broken vow,
My vows unpaid, how shall I dare
To hope that Thou wilt hear my prayer?

I do not come in my own name,
No right have I to make a claim,
Jesus, my Advocate, doth plead,
O Jesus, to the Father lead.

Again I knock at mercy's door,
Again I crave at mercy's store,
Canst Thou still give Thy grace to me,
Though I have been untrue to Thee?

My dead works on my conscience lie,
O'er broken bonds with tears I sigh,

O may the blood of Christ atone,
And cleanse my heart for Thee alone,

Though I have grieved Thee in the past,
Though my vows were too weak to last,
Yet rather than my Lord deny,
I feel I would for Jesus die.

What shall I render, Lord, to Thee
For all Thy benefits to me?
O help me on this holy day,
Fresh vows to make, and old ones pay.

Thy mercies now my heart constrain
To cov'nant with my Lord again;
O may this newest cov'nant be
Enduring as eternity.

Seal Thou my heart with love Divine,
Take all I have for ever Thine,
And let my daily life reveal
The imprint of Thy royal seal.

HOYLAKE,
   First Sunday, 1873.

"MORS JANUA VITÆ."
OR,
"DEATH THE GATE OF LIFE."

Composed after seeing the celebrated painting by Sir J. NOEL PATON.

With vision rapt I saw
  A soldier of the cross,
And full of sacred awe
  Beheld him count the loss
Of the hard fight, and reckon all the spoil.

"If the great world I gain,
   E'en though it be the whole,
 The bargain were in vain,
   I lose my priceless soul
And die a bankrupt after all my toil.

"Pleasant to carnal lust
   Sin's worldly gain may be,
 But shall I dare to trust
   Its subtle flattery,
And crave its wares though valuable they seem?
   I win a tempting prize,
     But lose it ere 'tis drawn,
   'Twill vanish from my eyes,
     And, my lost soul in pawn,
No price can then the fearful pledge redeem.

"Christ bids me to deny
   Myself from day to day,
 And on His grace rely,
   Though rough the heavenward way;
Fight the good fight of faith and thus lay hold
   Upon eternal life,
     And win the victor's crown,
   Pass from the heated strife,
     And on His throne sit down,
His everlasting glory to behold.

  ✣ ✣ ✣ ✣ ✣ ✣ ✣ ✣

"Welcome the cross, I take
   It up, and humbly bear
 It for my Master's sake;
   He bore a larger share
Of pain,—His cross was heavier than mine.
   With Him I suffer now,
     With Him I soon shall reign,

To Him my heart I bow;
"'Lord cleanse it from all stain
Of wilful sin, and make it pure like Thine.'"

○   ○   ○   ○   ○   ○   ○   ○

Look in the hottest front
  Of battle, where the brave
Bear manfully the brunt,
  And the tempest'ous wave
Of warfare rolls like the fierce surging sea;
  Gath'ring its crimson tide,
    Advancing more and more,
  Till in full swell of pride
    It breaks upon the shore,
And spends its life-flood in eternity.

With helm and sword and shield,
  Well clad in suit of mail,
His weapons he doth wield
  With valour to prevail,
As though his single arm a host had been.
  The struggle is severe,
    And e'en his well-scarred face
  Which knows no craven fear,
    Ennobled by the grace
Of bravery, blanched in the strife is seen.

The favour of his God
  He strongly seeks to win,
"Resisting unto blood
  And striving against sin,"
All honour gives where it alone is due.
  He royally maintains
    God to be all in all,
  Daily he conquest gains,
    Daily his foes do fall,
And his free heart to God is ever true.

Fainting yet firm he rests
 Upon his trusty blade,
When in his armoured breast
 He sees an awful shade,
Reflected from the low'ring outspread wing
 Of the last foe of all,
 The angel-dread of death;
 Chilled by the herald's pall,
 The brave man pants for breath,
But boldly cries, "O death, where is thy sting?"

The angel leads him through
 A valley dark and lone,—
Earth vanishes from view,
 He hears the hopeless moan,
Yet steadfastly he paces Death's domain;
 Sees Death in terrors robed,
 Hears tempters threaten still
 Ere he pass Death's abode
 His precious life to spill,
And swear by hell no refuge he shall gain.

Feeble, he follows now
 With barely room to tread,
And on his stricken brow
 As he moves near the dead,
Appears the latest passion of his soul.
 Death spreading his dark wing
 In dissolution's hour,
 Unsheaths his fatal sting,
 And in one stroke of power
Puts all his strength, and makes him feel the
 whole.

 Touched by the angel-guide,
 As though a cruel dart

By skilful archer plied
　　Shot through his quiv'ring heart,
Stirring the pangs of mortal agony.
　　Hard by an open grave
　　　　His strength begins to sink,
　　No human friend can save,
　　　　He yields upon the brink,
But gasps, "O grave, where is thy victory?"

　　Dropping his bruiséd helm,
　　　　His sword and beaten shield,
　　Closed in by Death's dark realm,
　　　　No light as yet revealed
To show the way beyond the yawning grave.
　　Hush! listen to his plea,
　　　　"For me the Saviour died,
　　My Lord I look to Thee,
　　　　No other trust beside,
I rest upon Thy grace alone to save."

　　While thus he bows in prayer,
　　　　With outstretched pleading hands;
　　Clad in a beauty rare
　　　　The noble angel stands,
Transformed into a herald radiant.
　　He turns a veil aside,
　　　　Reveals the "Gate of Life,"
　　Now robed as royal guide
　　　　To lead from mortal strife,
And beams with pity on the suppliant.

　　The colours of the bow
　　　　In pure transparent rays,
　　Melt in harmonious glow,
　　　　And shed immortal grace
Upon the warrior's rapt countenance.

The flood of liquid light
   Shows the brave man death-strick'n,
But kindling his dim sight
   With the deep bliss of heav'n
Blends with dying anguish joy triumphant.

O for a seraph's wing
   To veil our feeble eyes
In presence of the King,
   And see the glorious prize
Bestowed upon the saint, and see him crowned;
   Crowned, for the strife is done,
     Crowned in his Captain's name,
   Crowned for the conquest's won,
     Crowned with his Lord to reign.

  *   *   *   *   *   *   *   *

The veil is down.—Within the harpers sound.

HOYLAKE,
   January, 1873.

A MORNING HYMN.

My God, my Father, while I raise
My heart in early songs of praise,
Lift up Thy holy face in light
And scatter all the shades of night.

Sun of Eternal Life now shine
And fill my soul with beams Divine,
Let nothing in my mind remain
That is untrue, or dark, or vain.

In holy fellowship with Thee
No cloud of darkness can there be,
Light in the trusting heart shall spring,
And pure abiding joy shall bring.

Thy smile shall be my break of day,
Thy hand shall lead me on my way,
Thy favour shall enrich my heart,
And daily be my better part.

Thy Word shall be my constant law,
Thy presence my affections draw,
So shall my humble love be Thine,
And Thy unchanging love be mine.

Save me from all perplexing care,
And for my duties Lord, prepare,
Gird me with strength that I may prove
While in the world my faith and love.

Engaged amidst its toil and strife,
Fain would I earn the "Bread of Life,"
And thus secure a lasting store
When I can work on earth no more.

If busy for this life I be,
May I have perfect peace in Thee,
Hold forth Thy Word that men may know
My service is not all below.

Though I have earthly work to do,
I would fulfil the heavenly, too,
O suffer not my thought to swerve,
That Thee, and Thee alone, I serve.

There is another world than this,
A world of endless life and bliss,
A daily meetness may I gain
In that pure world with Thee to reign.

HOYLAKE.
March, 1873.

AN EVENING HYMN.

O God, my thankful heart would bring
Its loving homage while I sing;
I bless Thee that throughout the day,
Thou hast sustained me on my way.

I thank Thee for the light I've seen,
And for the comfort Thou hast been;
As all my days have passed before,
So this is crowned with mercy's store.

I thank Thee for my daily bread,
Thou hast in peace my spirit fed,
O grant in calm of eventide
To me the shelter of Thy side.

I thank Thee for my life and strength,
My hope of reaching heav'n at length,
That each day brings me nearer still
The mansions of Thy holy hill.

Help me to prove myself with care,
If I be fit to enter there;
If not, O Lord, now grant to me
More grace and heartfelt purity.

If I have grieved Thee, Lord, to day,
If negligence has marked my way,
If secret wrong hath entered in,
For Jesu's sake forgive my sin.

O make me simple as a child,
Happy because my Father smiled;
Finding a heaven in Thy love,
And meetness for the home above.

Let Thy love like a magnet be,
To draw my spirit near to Thee,
And when my days on earth shall end
Be Thou my everlasting Friend.

Watch o'er me in the hours of night,
Secure I lie beneath Thy sight;
O soothe me that I calmly rest
As infants on a mother's breast.

Bless me again, Lord, bless me now,
Deepen Thy seal upon my brow,
And let the bright and royal sign
Declare to all that I am Thine.

HOYLAKE,
    March, 1873.

A GREAT SORROW.

FIRST PART.

THE WAIL.

O! my heart, art thou not broken,
  Since thy sorrows are so sore?
Sorrows which no tongue hath spoken,
  Sorrows I ne'er felt before.

O! my heart thou canst not find
  Treasure such as thou hast lost;
O'er thy loss my stricken mind
  Is in wild confusion tossed.

O! my heart, thy springing life
  Is all withered in thy pain;
Nor in thy tumult'ous strife
  Can it ever grow again.

SONGS IN TRIAL.

O! my heart, canst thou survive,
   Now thy roots are torn away?
Is it worth for life to strive
   Now dark night spreads o'er thy day?

O! my heart is worn and weary,
   For its load is great to bear,
And the path I tread is dreary,
   Nought to comfort anywhere.

O! my heart, I feel thee bleed,
   Anguish tears thee with its throbs,
All thy life faints in its need,
   All thy voice hushed in its sobs.

O! my heart, I look in vain
   For a balm to heal thy grief;
Comfort fleeth from thy pain,
   Earth can give thee no relief.

O! my heart, thy depths are filled
   With a bitter portion now;
Every joy thou hadst is spilled,
   And thy anguish wrings my brow.

O! my heart, thou helpless thing,
   Sinking in my troubled breast,
Nothing near where thou canst cling,
   Nothing near where thou canst rest.

O! my heart, the deep'ning gloom
   Gathers round thee like a pall,
And I seem to tread the tomb,
   Shiv'ring at my own footfall.

! my heart, thy bitter wail
 Moves the pity of my God;
His Divine help cannot fail,
 Though He smite thee with His rod.

SECOND PART.
THE PRAYER.

O! my God, no hope have I
 Till Thou bring it to my heart;
All my hope is drained and dry,
 My soul to the quick doth smart.

O! my God, a feeble spark
 Flickers in my clouded soul;
Wilt Thou fan it ere the dark
 Shadows quench it as they roll?

O! my God, this heart of mine
 Is a weak and shattered thing;
Wilt Thou draw it, Lord, to Thine,
 Heal its wounds beneath Thy wing?

O! my God, the storm is wild,
 Thy great love must feel for me;
Save Thy wrecked and sinking child,
 Let me now some shelter see.

O! my God, if Thou canst give
 Life back to the buried dead;
Then a dying one may live,
 And a heart may heal that bled.

O! my God, Thou seest me lie
 Restless on an awful brink;
If Thou leave me I shall die,
 If Thou loose me I shall sink.

O! my God, this fierce despair
    Flings me on a barren waste,
Wilt Thou see me perish there?
    Father, to my rescue haste!

O! my God, if hope be gone,
    If there shine no star for me,
Then, a lost and lonely one,
    Let me perish near to Thee.

O! my God, my heart is cold,
    Draw me closer to Thy breast;
Let me in Thy love behold
    For my restless soul a rest.

O! my God, yet will I hope
    Mercy hath not gone from Thee;
Though in darkness still I grope
    For Thine hand outstretched to me.

O! my God, forsake me not,
    Though my life Thou dost bereave,
Thou shalt still control my lot,
    Thou wilt ne'er Thy servant leave.

THIRD PART.

THE REST.

Rest, my soul, the shadows flee;
    Welcome, welcome, is the dawn!
Weeping through the night may be,
    But joy cometh with the morn.

Rest, my soul, may richer fruit
    Be the harvest of thy pain,

Though the pruning was acute,
    Sweeter produce shall remain.

Rest, my soul, thy portion now
    Is in the eternal King;
To His blessed will I bow,
    To His constant love I cling.

Rest, my soul, be not afraid,
    God will shield thee from all harm;
None thy refuge shall invade,
    None disturb thy sacred calm.

Rest, my soul, thou'st borne the cross,
    Jesus smiles upon thee now,
He doth recompense thy loss
    With the sunlight of His brow.

Rest, my soul, a richer prize
    Than the world can give to thee,
Glitters in the brighter skies
    Of a pure eternity.

Rest, my soul, if thou hast given
    Dearer sacrifice than life,
When, at length, I enter heaven,
    God will not forget thy strife.

Rest, my soul, the vale of tears
    Leads me to my home above,
Hushed for ever be my fears,
    In the depths of Jesu's love.

Rest, my soul, thine ark is sure,
    Though on raging billows cast,
It shall ev'ry storm endure,
    And the haven reach at last.

Rest, my soul, I can not tell
　What my Father may intend,
But He hath done all things well,
　And He will do to the end.

LONDON,
　April, 1873.

O, LIGHT IS SWEET!

O, LIGHT is sweet!
　At early dawn,
With joy we greet
　The bright'ning morn;
When lonesome night hath wove its shadows dense,
　And drawn them round us like a gloomy veil,
Leaving us helpless in our own defence
　Till merry sunbeams midnight shadows scale,
　　With nimble feet
　　And laughing eye
　　Skip o'er the sky;
　　O, light is sweet!

O, light is sweet!
　When darkness frowned,
And fierce storms beat
　The cringing ground,
And lurid lightnings like bright burnished darts,
　Cleft the wild tempest with a giant's might.
His fi'ry anger glancing to our hearts,
　Hath made us tremble at the awful sight,
　　But gentle feet
　　Behind his back,

Have smoothed his track;
O, light is sweet!

O, light is sweet!
When shining hours
With radiance meet
The op'ning flowers,
And bid the prince of beauties not to shrink
But with a fragrant modesty disclose,
While pearly dew-drops melt upon its brink,
The native splendours of the blushing rose.
"O, light is sweet!"
"In nature's bowers;"
So sing the flowers,
"O, light is sweet!"

O, light is sweet!
When in the cell
With fettered feet
As though in hell,
The captive chafes and frets in midnight gloom,
Nursing a vengeance in his angry soul,
Like a lost spirit in its hopeless doom;
But e'en in his dark heart the morning stole
Where passions beat,
And seemed to say,
"Kneel down to pray."
O, light is sweet!

O, light is sweet!
When on the raft
Wild billows beat
The hapless craft
Which weary mariners, from sinking wreck,
Have lashed together to outride the sea,

Their eager watches eastern sunbeams beck,
  In hope that help may come to set them free;
     Help! Help be fleet,
     If thou canst save
     From wat'ry grave;
      O, light is sweet!

     O, light is sweet!
      On trackless waste;
     With blistered feet
      The trav'ller's haste
Carries him further in the wilds astray,
  Until the dreadful feeling comes, lost, lost!
With all his heart he looks and prays for day,
  And could he buy it, would give any cost;
     His cries repeat
     Yet more and more
     Than e'er before,
      "O, light is sweet!"

     O, light is sweet!
      When on his bed
     With fev'rish heat
      And aching head
The suff'rer lies racked in his sleepless pain,
  And anxiously full oft he gasps for morn;
Even to him fresh slumber comes again
  In the mild moments of the springing dawn.
     O, it is meet
     To let him sleep,
     And though we weep,
      The light is sweet!

     O, light is sweet!
      When sinners bend

    At Mercy's seat,
     And seek a friend
To ease their guilty conscience of its pain;
 Like as a wounded deer pants for the stream,
When mortal anguish doth its life-blood drain;
 O what a blessed refuge it doth seem
    At Jesu's feet,
     Where love Divine
     Begins to shine;
      O, light is sweet!

     O, light is sweet!
      Unto the heart,
     Whose piteous bleat
      And pungent smart
Bespeak the presence of an inward grief,
 Which cast out peace and in its room hath dwelt;
The mourner seeks but findeth no relief,
 With hope so long deferred, heart-sick he felt.
     But, when complete,
      God's chast'ning plan,
     The stricken man
      Sings, "Light is sweet!"

     O, light is sweet!
      To dying saint
     For heaven meet,
      But weak and faint
In final conflict with the mortal foe;
 Death aims full well his penetrating dart,
And casting all his strength into the blow
 Drives it into his victim's quiv'ring heart.

  ✦ ✦ ✦ ✦ ✦ ✦ ✦ ✦

In winding sheet
  The body lies,
The spirit cries
  "O, light is sweet!"

LONDON,
  May, 1873.

THE DISAPPOINTED SOWER.

THE fallow ground
  Spread far around,
And lab'rers here and there
  Went forth to sow,
  And broadcast throw
The seed with tears and prayer.

The master sent
  His men who spent
Their strength upon the field,
  But precious seed
  Was choked with weed
And barren in the yield.

Bad was the soil,
  And great the toil
The furrows to prepare,
  The lab'rers few,
  And feeble too,
To do much culture there.

The stubborn clod
  So hard was trod,
The ploughshare bright and keen

Was roughly spurned,
And hardly turned
A furrow on the scene.

The rock was there
To spoil the care
With which the seed was sown;
It sprung full soon
But heat of noon
The blade scorched to the stone.

But plots were found
Of better ground
In which the soil was deep;
So workman heed,
Bring here your seed
If you desire to reap.

Yet even here,
Where ground was clear
And good in workmen's eyes,
The seed oft lay,
Many a day,
As though it ne'er would rise.

A sower cast
The good seed fast,
The sweat broke on his brow,
His busy hand
Bestrewed the land
With harvest to endow.

When he had done
He watched the sun
And show'rs refresh the ground;

  As if he thought
  The sowing ought
At once to spring around.

  He quite forgot
  It was the lot
Of seed to lie unseen
  Through months of time,
  Before the prime
Of harvest life was green.

  The sower fain
  Would look again
Into the earth to see
  If seed did spring,
  And promise bring
Of ripe maturity.

  He waited long
  Amid the throng
Of workers in the field,
  With drooping mind
  He sat and pined
Because it did not yield.

  One troubled day,
  On king's highway,
He mourned the lack of sheaves,
  His care and cost
  Were labour lost,
He thought, and so he grieves.

  His bitter tears
  And deeper fears
For hope left little room,

'Twas sad to see
One such as he
Thus yearn for harvest bloom.

   o   o   o   o   o

But now it seems
That sweating teams
Are toiling up this way,
  Filling the roads
  With harvest loads,
And storing all the day.

"Whence comes the wain
  With all this grain?"
The drooping sower asked;
  "'Tis from thy land
  And of thy hand,"
The reaper said and passed.

He asked once more,
"Whence comes this store?
Are these sheaves thine or mine?"
  "What thou hast sown,
  That I have mown,
So 'tis both mine and thine."

Yet others came
Who said the same,
"Fruit of thy seed we bring;
  Give us thine hand
  And join our band
While harvest home we sing."

They all agreed
Without his seed
No harvest could have been;

While he had wept
The seed which slept
So long, was duly seen.

With joy they met
The man who set
The harvest in the ground;
"Lift up thy voice,"
They cried, "Rejoice,"
"What thou hadst lost we found."

"Give God the praise,
For He doth raise
The seed with large increase;
Though long it lay,
We reap to day,
And garner it in peace."

HOYLAKE,
   March, 1873.

THE PHYSICIAN'S WAITING ROOM.

CALMLY we wait around,
  Yet in some hearts are found
Secrets of anxious thought, which lie unknown,
  Save in the owner's breast,
  Where they too deeply rest,
And to Divine Omniscience on the throne.

  Hard by is human skill,
  Whose touch on mortal ill
We crave, and yet for power more potent call;

Though not expressed in word
The silent prayer is heard,
And moves the Great Physician above all.

Swift as a beam of light,
Or e'en electric flight,
Answers of peace are given to the soul;
And ministries Divine
Our anxious hearts incline
To cast all care on Him that bears the whole.

If then the skill we seek,
Though great, alas! be weak,
To meet the needs of our infirmity;
Yet One there doth remain
To ease our heartfelt pain,
Who ever liveth in eternity.

Teach me to do Thy will,
So I may best fulfil
O Lord the duty Thou hast laid on me;
Whate'er I seek in means,
If Thy will intervenes,
I would deny myself to honour Thee.

LONDON,
May, 1873.

The following lines were suggested as the writer stood by the Martyrs' Memorial Stone in Smithfield, London. The inscription is copied from the stone.

> "Within a few feet of this spot
> JOHN ROGERS,
> JOHN BRADFORD,
> JOHN PHILPOT,
> And other servants of God,
> suffered death by fire for the
> faith of Christ,
> In the years 1555, 1556, 1557."

Do I now gaze upon the stain
Where faithful martyrs have been slain?
And was it here they braved the stake
As witnesses for Jesu's sake?
Here they were bound in red-hot chains,
Here that they suffered mortal pains,
Here they endured the bigot's fire
Rather than take the traitor's hire
Their Lord and Saviour to disown,
And bring dishonour to His throne?
Here that with life they freely sealed
The truth Jehovah hath revealed?
Accounting it an honour given
To testify and die for heaven,
Holding the truth a greater prize
Than any of their earthly ties,
Wives, children, friends, forsaking all
In answer to their Master's call;
Not with fanatic haste, but well
And wisely counted cost to tell,
The Word of God could ne'er be bound,
Nor ought could shake the holy ground,—

Priests, Kings, and Councils, or the Pope—
In which the anchor of their hope
Was strong, and sure within the veil
Where persecution's fiercest gale
Could never loosen its firm hold,
Never! though angry billows rolled,
And deep cried hoarsely unto deep,
And angry passions would not sleep;
Unfathomable depths were shown
And beaten wrecks on rocks were thrown,
Never, e'en then, could they be moved
From Him whom they believed and loved.

O God, we bless Thee for the grand,
Faithful, triumphant, martyred band;
Their ashes 'neath Thine altar lie,
Aloud their awful voices cry,
How long, O holy Lord! how long
Shall men dispute the right with wrong?
Deny, with unbelief and lies,
That which alone can make them wise,
And pure, and good, and fit to be
In happy company with Thee?
Alone, uproot and cast away
The sins which stain them ev'ry day,
And make their hearts a temple bright
Where nothing shall offend Thy sight,
But radiant with Thy glory shine,
And burning with Thy love Divine?
Thankful that Smithfield fires are spent,
We bless Thee peaceful times are sent;
But never let us in this land
Shrink to maintain a Christian stand;
Never disown in ease or pride
The truth for which the martyrs died.

SONGS IN TRIAL.

Shall we esteem God's word the less,
In heart believe and not confess;
Our conscience telling us it's true,
Our practice hiding it from view;
Strive to be all things to all men,
Pray with the Church of Christ, and then
Go out into the busy world
Bearing the gospel banner furled,
Or leave it secretly at home,
That none may trace us as we roam
A little just on mammon's side,
The breach not making very wide?
Just near enough the gospel door
An extra stretch will bridge it o'er;
Dropping into our Master's cup,
Of mammon's draught a little sup,
Only a drop or two to taste:
A pity worldly bliss to waste
By being scrupulous or nice,
When offered at so low a price.
When such a bargain why not buy?
To make ends meet may we not try
And serve both masters if we can?
Alas! Is this a Christian man?
O heaven let the martyr's cry
Ring loudly from the open sky,
Hypocrisy shall fear and quake;
And all who name Thy name shall wake
And brace themselves, with purpose strong,
To spread the cry,—O Lord! how long?
With sworn and everlasting vow
Their energy to Thee shall bow,
And men shall be firm as the cross,
Nor fearing earthly scorn or loss.

Devils may tempt, and fools may sneer,
But perfect love shall cast out fear,
And though the world seduce and smile,
Its arts shall ne'er again beguile.
Mammon shall henceforth bribe in vain,
Its gold may glitter, but its gain
Shall leave behind no guilty brand
To stain the consecrated hand,
Nor ought Thy witnesses shall shame
To hide again Thy royal name.

LONDON,
  May, 1873.

A SONG.

Awake, awake, my weary heart,
  Thou shalt not droop and die,
For thou hast now a royal part
  With multitudes on high.

O wake! and sing a grateful song,
  Arise above thy cares,
Thy sorrows may have lasted long,
  But God thy burden bears.

If rough the path which thou hast trod,
  If rougher still before,
And strength thou needest from Thy God,
  He now will give thee more.

Rugged and steep may be the way,
  But grace Divine is free,

SONGS IN TRIAL.

Sufficient unto ev'ry day,
　Sufficient unto thee.

Jehovah's everlasting arm
　Is all around thee still,
And thou shalt feel a holy calm
　While bending to His will.

On Him thou mayest daily lean,
　Yea, lean with all thy load,
For His omnipotence hath been
　Thy staff upon the road.

No foe that mighty staff can break,
　O! rest on it anew;
God's strength is pledged for Jesu's sake
　Till heaven appear in view.

Nor will He leave thee at its gate,
　To gaze without, alone,
But share with thee His rich estate,
　And place thee on His throne.

HOYLAKE,
　August, 1873.

THE LORD'S SONG,

How shall I sing Jehovah's song
　Lone in a foreign land?
My exiled harp unstrung, hath long
　Been silent in my hand.

Fain would I brace its feeble strings,
　And tune it o'er again,

But in so strange a land it rings
    Alas! of heartfelt pain.

Yet will I touch my harp and try
    The old inspiring theme,
It may be God will hear on high,
    Though played by Bab'lon's stream.

O God! the touch is somewhat strange,
    Yet does it sound like home,
Nor would I murmur at the change,
    If for Thy sake I roam.

Thy presence can, in ev'ry land,
    Provide a rest for me,
Give power and freedom to my hand
    To play a song for Thee.

O grant me now Thy Israel's skill
    A harmony to sound,
With hallowed inspiration fill,
    Let faith and love abound.

Then shall I tread the tempter down,
    Then shall my heart be free,
Then shall I win the fadeless crown
    Thou holdest forth to me.

Yea, now a greater strength I gain,
    Yea, now a sweeter cheer,
Thy song I do not sing in vain,
    For Thou art truly near.

HOYLAKE,
    August, 1873.

MY FATHER'S GRAVE.

RURAL it lies before my eyes,
    Marked by a marble stone,
The spot is fair, but is it there
    My Father lies alone?

I see it now, beneath the bough
    Of an o'erspreading tree;
And as I gaze, the former days
    Rise up in memory.

The buoyant life which in the strife
    Of earthly duties done,
Yet sought the light of God's pure sight,
    And blest the rising sun.

Depressing shade was rarely laid
    Across the path he trod,
Though trial came it brought no shame,
    For he had peace with God.

The spirit mild, which, like a child,
    Found joy in simple things,
And revelled where no carnal care
    Dissatisfaction brings.

The cheerful voice which would rejoice
    The hearts of those around,
And e'er incite a pure delight
    The world ne'er sought or found.

The father's heart, in ev'ry part,
    So tender wise and true,

Parental care was ever there,
  And guile it never knew.

The earnest soul, where used to roll
  The fount of Christian love,
The gushing stream would often seem
  Replenished from above.

The manly grace, the open face,
  The frank and beaming eye,
The hoary head, the solid tread,
  These mem'ries never die.

They live and last until the past
  Seems present o'er again,
And we forget he slumbers yet,
  Unseen by mortal men.

Yea, higher rise, beyond the skies
  To the immortal just,
For earthly mould doth merely hold
  Its kin the mortal dust.

And e'en his dust is in the trust
  Of Christ, until the hour
When it shall rise, the honoured prize
  Of His redeeming power.

Then shall we pause and weep because
  The grave hath his remains?
Nay on its brink we rather think
  That he with Jesus reigns.

SHARDLOW,
  July, 1873.

BATTLE.

Wild is the storm, the tempest raves
And roars in madd'ning winds and waves;
Its utmost fury is let loose,
No interval of calm or truce,
But fierce and stern determined battle:
The arrows in its quiver rattle,
Its bow is held with giant strength,
And ev'ry dart drawn to its length;
Hissing they cleave the quiv'ring sky,
Unswerving to their goal they fly,
Shaft after shaft is buried deep,
And life is changed for death's hard sleep.
Yet no remorse the tempest knows,
Nor pities nature in her woes;
Heedless of weather-beaten men
Who shelter in the dripping den,
All hoping, till they all despair,
In misery they linger there.
The passions of the storm increase,
Rejecting ev'ry plea for peace.
The forest trees of hoary age
Are scathed and riven in its rage,
Uprooted by the cruel blast,
Their glory is for ever past;
Upon the ground they prostrate lie,
Where once they towered to the sky;
Their massive trunks are basely torn,
Their graceful branches rudely shorn,
And all the chaste and silken life
Of foliage withered in the strife,—
The precious growth of many years
The tempest, in a moment, shears.

Its cry is, havoc! havoc still!
Its fury now will have its fill;
Heaving the ocean to its deeps,
And casting into fearful steeps
Its waters, seething more and more,
Like a huge cauldron boiling o'er;
Flinging afar its angry flakes,
Till e'en the bravest mariner quakes.
His vessel shivers to the keel,
And staggers with a drunken reel
As though besotted in the strife,
And mocking at both death and life.
Its stately masts so strong and tall
Come crashing with an awful fall.
Its ragged rigging chokes the deck,
Until a shattered helpless wreck
It drifts upon the rock-bound coast,
And ev'ry soul on board is lost.
The greedy tempest claims its prey,
And death acknowledges its sway.
Fierce in its rage, but fiercer still,
The storm which lashes human will,
Rouses in the immortal soul
Wild billows, deeper in their roll.
Strong passions beat with surging swell,
As furiously stirred by hell.
A dart is rankling in the breast,
And conscience in its guilt can't rest,
Anger and unbelief are there,
And self-will stifles ev'ry prayer,
Pride true obedience disdains,
And dark temptation only reigns.
'Tis Belial's malignant hour,
The tempter triumphs in his power;

Fain would he end the strife, and kill
Body and soul to glut his will.
O! minist'ring angels, where are ye?
This mental conflict haste to see,
And if ye may, some heav'nly balm
Drop from your wings and bring a calm.
Befriend the agitated heart,
And in its trouble take its part;
Cherish its feeble languid vows,
Its better principles arouse,
Impart new strength to keep at bay,
Yea, drive its enemies away.
Breathe sympathy into the soul,
'Till heaven hath well inspired the whole,
Immanuel supreme proclaim,
And plant the banner in His name.
O Jesus, Master, in this hour
Of battle, let Thy voice of power
Speak as the Prince of truth and peace,
And bid this hard fought conflict cease.
Cast down the tempter's evil throne,
And magnify Thy right alone
To rule, with royalty Divine,
And make the human heart like Thine;
No pride, or discord, or self-will,
But all within so pure and still,
That God may be distinctly heard,
Nor ought oppose His ruling word.
Its homage to Jehovah bound,
Its pleasure in His favour found,
Its duty learned from God the Son,
" Father not my will, Thine be done."

HOYLAKE,
    August, 1873.

THE PILGRIM'S NIGHT SONG.

The sunlight is fading,
    The road is so dreary,
The darkness is shading
    My path, and I'm weary;
O heavenly Guide, wilt Thou give me Thine hand?
Thou only shalt lead me while in this strange land.

I wait for the morning,
    But I'm sometimes afraid
That ere it is dawning
    I shall sink in the shade,
But if I do fail still my Lord is with me,
And a merciful Judge I know He will be.

Though faint, I'm pursuing,
    For my goal is before,
In weakness enduring,
    But a rest is in store;
Each step of my travel brings nearer the close,
Then after the journey how sweet the repose.

I am often perplexed
    But I never despair,
Though temptation hath vexed
    Me, I cast all my care
Where I know there is power my load to sustain,
And love to refresh me whatever my pain.

In Thy mighty guiding
    How can danger befall?
In Thee I'm confiding,
    For no evil at all

Can hide the bright beaming which flows from Thy
    face,
With Thee ever shining I trust if not trace.

    All my doubts drive away,
      My feeble heart strengthen,
    Lead by night and by day,
      Then shadows may lengthen,
And every step of the road be unknown,
Still in faith I shall walk with Thee to Thy throne.

HOYLAKE,
    August, 1873.

THE ANGEL OF HOPE.

    HAIL! holy Angel,
      Spread Thy pinions bright,
    May Thine evangel
      Bring me purer light;
O wing Thy welcome way into my breast,
And soothe my ruffled spirit into rest.

    Break the hard fetter
      Which enchains my heart,
    And give me better
      Thoughts, to heal the smart
Of my bruised soul, now on temptation's brink,
Which, but for Thee, in its dark depths would sink.

    The tempter hath flung
      Himself in my way,

And conflict hath wrung
    My spirit to pray:
Blest Angel now smite him, and backward roll
His legions, whose arrows have scathed my soul.

Thou seest his snare
    With subtlety planned,
But with Thee I dare
    Defy his bold hand;
Thy glittering shield shall cover me well,
And drive all my enemies back into hell.

O Angel Divine,
    Direct from above,
No merit of mine
    Hath won Thy great love,
Yet in Thy free gift there's something to spare;
To strengthen my heart when burdened with care.

My spirit upraise,
    'Tis soiled in the dust,
O teach me to praise,
    And help me to trust;
For though I have oft been nigh to despair,
Thou never could'st leave me to perish there.

When no other friend
    Is near to my side,
Thou succour dost send,
    And with me abide;
Through ev'ry dark cloud Thy smile I behold
Regilding the sky more richly than gold.

In dead of the night
    There's ever Thy star,

To shed its clear light
  And guide me afar,
Its beautiful shining seemeth to say,
Fear not the darkness it soon will be day.

HOYLAKE,
   August, 1873.

WHEN I FEEL THAT LIFE IS LONELY.

When I feel that life is lonely,
  When I think that it is sad,
When, of all my friends, One only
  Can make my dull spirit glad.

When I feel that hope is waning,
  When I fear that it is gone,
When, in all my prospects, gaining
  Guiding light from only One.

When the storm is wildly beating,
  When I hear it sigh and moan,
When, of all my helpers meeting,
  Refuge is in One alone.

When my harassed soul is fretting
  O'er the tempter's subtle snare,
When I seek relief, but getting
  Not a comfort anywhere.

Then the mighty One revealing
  Tender sympathy with me,
And though yet escape concealing,
  Surely makes my spirit free.

Blessed be the One abiding,
    Blessed be His open door,
In His goodness still confiding,
    Let me learn to love Him more.

HOYLAKE,
    August, 1873.

THE WOUNDED SOLDIER'S OUT-LOOK.

O HEAVEN! a wounded soldier prays,
    Wilt Thou his pleading heed?
O heaven, bless the tender heart,
The hands which take the healing part,
    Of the Samaritan's deed.

O bless the love which sought me out
    Like the great Friend of friends;
The healing oil is sweeter still,
Because it comes with such free will,
    And true compassion blends.

My wounds are easier to bear
    While sympathy is near;
And if I sicken or I die,
Great Captain let Thy servant lie
    Where he the fight may hear.

Next to the glory of the strife,
    'Tis glorious to be
Wounded upon the battle field,
And see and hear my comrades wield
    Their strength and life for Thee.

O comrades, stand ye all like men,
    And make the foeman fly;
How little should I think of pain,
While many valiant still remain
    Ready to dare and die.

If unbelievers truth deny
    And some weak spirits fail,
No matter who may stand or fall,
'Tis not a doubtful fight at all,
    Truth does and shall prevail.

The issues of the conflict leave,
    Heaven will avenge its loss,
And let your steady purpose aim
To do God's will, as He who came
    To do it on the cross.

Let not a selfish thought of praise
    Your strong arm paralyse,
For if in human strength ye trust,
Your banner shall be trailed in dust
    From which it cannot rise.

Let not a mere desire to win
    Be in your battle cry;
Let ev'ry one be at his post,
Though devils threaten all the host,
    And many brave men lie

Disabled on their battered shields,
    And bearing mortal scars;
Yet e'en while life is ebbing fast,
They watch ye to the very last,
    Till borne in vict'ry's cars

To hear their noble Captain say
  "Ye have your duty done:
Let each receive his promised crown,
And, full of holy zeal, look down
  Till the grand conquest's won.

"The foe is bound—I hold his chain,
  Satan and hell shall see
That all who have My glory sought,
I glory for them, too, have bought,
  Eternal life with Me."

HOYLAKE,
  August, 1873.

OUR MOTHER'S BIRTHDAY.

DEAR mother, 'tis thy natal day,
  How many years art thou?
Dost tire of life's uneven way,
  Or art thou weary now?

Dost feel the weight of coming age,
  Dost think thy life is spun,
That short is now thy pilgrimage,
  Thy mother's duty done?

Dost think that there is little left
  To keep thee ling'ring here,
Already of so much bereft,
  That nought remains to cheer?

Nay, thou hast loving children still,
  And children's children too,

And if thou canst not now fulfil
    What thou hast used to do,

Thy children do not love thee less
    Than they have done before,
But all with true affection bless
    And cherish thee the more.

The silver of thy glist'ning hair
    Is to thy children dear,
And easier lies their load of care
    Whilst their good mother's near.

Thy precious life is more to them
    Than any earthly gold,
And years are but a diadem
    To crown thee when thou'rt old.

Thy presence, like a loom of power,
    Weaves all thy children's love,
And the warm robe shall be thy dower,
    Till thou art robed above.

They gather dignity from thee,
    They warm their love by thine,
And daily shall their purpose be,
    To honour thy decline.

They love the outbeam of thine age,
    They love the soul within,
And noble purposes engage,
    An earnestness to win

A place in thy true mother's heart,
    That what they lose or gain,
Whate'er may gather or depart,
    Thy blessing may remain.

O daily may thy children's love
  Be more like love Divine,
Supremely pledged to God above,
  And then for ever thine.

But sweeter than our love can be
  Is that for which we call,
May God a Husband be to thee,
  A Father to us all.

HOYLAKE,
  September 1st, 1873.

ROCK OF AGES.

Rock of Ages! still I cling
  With a trusting heart to Thee,
And amid the storm I sing
  "Ever shall my refuge be,
In the cleft above the waves,
In the love which fully saves."

Though I hear the rising swell
  Of the tempest at Thy feet,
And the blasphemies of hell
  In their angry passions beat,
Casting unbelief and pride
On Thy sacred riven side:

Though I see with heartfelt pain
  Many wrecks around Thee lie,
And the sinking souls disdain
  All the succour which is nigh,

SONGS IN TRIAL.

Heedless in their dying day,
Drifting hopelessly away:

Rock of Ages! still I cling
   With a trusting heart to Thee,
And in gratitude I bring
   Now the oft-repeated plea,
"Let me all my life abide
In the refuge of Thy side."

Rock of Ages! let no foe
   Ever tempt me to depart,
Whither, whither can I go
   To repose my weary heart?
To Thy fount which doth alone
For my sinfulness atone.

Rock of Ages! let my hand
   Cleave to Thee with stronger hold,
Let my feet more firmly stand,
   Let my heart become more bold,
Let me reckon gain and loss
By the value of Thy cross.

Rock of Ages! let Thy peace
   Be the secret of my soul,
And though earthly cares increase,
   Thou can'st ev'ry one control,
How, beneath Thy tranquil shade,
Can I ever be afraid?

Rock of Ages! when I die
   Let my pillow be on Thee,
When a sufferer I lie,
   Let me on Thy summit see

Glory blending with Thy light,
Heaven coming into sight.

Rock of Ages! still I cling
　　With a trusting heart to Thee,
Life may fail, and death may sting,
　　But in all my hope shall be—
Evil cannot reach me here,
Faith hath conquest over fear.

HOYLAKE,
　　October, 1873.

MY FATHER, BLESS ME.

My FATHER bless me, though sinful I be,
Let me the light of Thy countenance see,
Let Thy favour be mine, my portion Divine,
My heart be Thy kingdom, and rule it as Thine.

My Father, I cry, help me to rely
On Thy changeless love which always is nigh,
By temptation distrest, I fly to Thy breast,
And there, like an innocent child, let me rest.

My Father, Thy hand leads me through a land,
'Tis toilsome to walk, and danger to stand,
But if Thou dost reveal, and impress Thy seal
On my weak trembling heart, what fear can I feel?

My Father, Thy will may be myst'ry still,
Yet what Thou bidd'st me I fain would fulfil.

If Thou dost not explain the cause of my pain,
I know that I never can trust Thee in vain.

My Father, in Thee my refuge shall be,
Though dark be my path yet light is in Thee,
For Thy goodness doth shine on me and on mine,
And whatever Thou dost I ought not repine.

My Father, I claim in Jesus's name,
Thy grace to preserve from sin and from shame,
Do Thou make my heart pure and strong to endure,
And daily may Jesus and heaven be sure.

My Father, I know Thou lov'st to bestow
Thy succour to save, for now it doth flow;
Help me ever to live the truth I believe,
Till, as joint-heir with Christ, a crown I receive.

LISCARD,
February, 1874.

A FAMILY SONG.

" FATHER which art in heaven,"
   Enthroned in power above,
Thou hast to us Thy mercies given,
   And blest us with Thy love.

A family we meet
   In thankfulness to sing,
And as we gather at Thy feet,
   Our cheerful homage bring.

Our earthly home we love,
    For Thou hast made it dear;
The promise of a home above,
    A little heaven here.

Thou hast from day to day
    Our constant need supplied,
Thou never hast sent us away
    Of any good denied.

Thou giv'st us living bread,
    And water from the spring,
At whose eternal Fountain Head,
    Afresh in faith we cling.

Unite us in that name
    Which is our guarantee,
That we shall ever prove the same
    Kind Fatherhood in Thee.

May each keep near the cross,
    May each Thy witness be,
And grant, whatever be our loss,
    O Lord we ne'er lose Thee.

O Jesus! may Thy care
    So rule our life and heart,
That in our Father's house we share
    An everlasting part.

LISCARD,
    February, 1874.

A MORNING SONG.

O God! I own Thy kingly sway,
And bless Thee for the light of day;
Thy power hath made the sun to shine,
Thy love enkindles light Divine.

'Tis sweet at morn to see the sun,
'Tis pleasant when the day is done,
But to the soul it's sweeter still
To catch the light from Zion's hill.

O God! Thou art the Fount of light,
Thy presence banishes the night,
Though shadows on my spirit fall,
No darkness is in Thee at all.

And Thou hast said that I may be
O God, my Father, like to Thee,
Foretasting of the joys above,
The spring of sacred light and love.

Lord, I look up; O Father, shine—
Let me now see Thy smile Divine;
Let me now feel I have a part,
Deep in my heavenly Father's heart.

Strong I begin the work of day,
Afresh pursue my pilgrim way,
A promise in Thy love I see
That as my days my strength shall be.

Liscard,
   March, 1874.

LORD, IS IT I?

Care, care, dark care
Lieth everywhere,
Who casteth its great load
Of hard stones on the road?
  Lord, is it I?
  O why, O why?

Pain, pain, keen pain
Cometh again,
Who thrusteth the sharp steel
Which in my heart I feel?
  Lord, is it I?
  O why, O why?

Fear, fear, weak fear
Seemeth so near,
Who letteth the foe in?
O is it my own sin?
  Lord, is it I?
  O why, O why?

Dust, dust, in dust
Droopeth my trust,
Who planteth the sly snare,
And entangleth me there?
  Lord, is it I?
  O why, O why?

Down, down, cast down
Under God's frown,
Who hath my Father grieved
And chastisement received?

Lord, is it I?
O why, O why?

Hope! hope! yet hope,
Lost heart look up!
Who is it in this hour
Speaks with such love and power?
 Lord, is it Thee?
 'Tis Thee, 'tis Thee.

EGREMONT,
 1874.

WRITTEN FOR A BEREAVED MOTHER.

A MOTHER had a flow'ret rare,
 'Twas precious in its birth,
She tended it with loving care,
 And could not tell its worth.

She placed the young bud in her heart,
 That it might nourished be,
And there fulfilled a mother's part
 With true fidelity.

The mother passed her garden through,
 And all her plants looked o'er;
The bud was choicest in her view,
 And richest of her store.

She watched its tender leaves unfold,
 So silken was their hue,

In her warm love afresh she rolled
　The flow'ret as it grew.

It struck its roots into her breast,
　Her life in its was bound,
And closer still the mother prest
　The treasure she had found.

The fragrance of the flow'ret filled
　The mother's inmost soul,
And, in return, her love instilled
　Itself into the whole.

But the great Husbandman on high,
　Loved the young flow'ret, too;
He saw it in her bosom lie
　And bore it from her view.

The mother's heart did nearly break,
　When the young bud was gone,
"O Lord, alone, for Thy dear sake,
　Could I give up this one."

The royal Husbandman looked down,
　And to the mother said,
"Thy bud is planted in My crown,
　The flow'ret is not dead.

"It liveth now; it is My will
　To rear the bud on high,
But it shall be thy flow'ret still,
　Though nourished in the sky."

"Let hope of heaven heal thy pain,
　My flow'rets thou shalt see,

And thou shalt have thy bud again
   When thou art come to Me."

HOYLAKE,
  January, 1873.

WORK.

O LET me take hold of the plough,
   O let me grip it again,
I would put my strength to it now,
   As I toil with working men.

Do I hold with a trembling hand
   And open furrow with care?
I joy in the smell of the land
   Which yields to the keen ploughshare.

O give me the hopper of seed,
   And a broadcast let me throw,
With an earnest heart in the deed,
   God loveth to have it so.

It springs! O it springs in the blade!
   And the blade into the ear,
Heaven hath a ripe harvest made,
   And calleth its sons to shear.

O give me the sickle of love,
   The sickle so bright and keen,
I reap for my Master above,
   And angels garner it in.

O God, I am working for Thee,
   I cheer my labour with song,
For richer my wages will be
   And rest is coming ere long.

Have I mingled sowing with tears,
   And waited long for the sheaves?
Now I say, " Begone," to my fears,
   The reaper his due receives.

EGREMONT,
   August, 1874.

www.ingramcontent.com/pod-product-compliance
Lightning Source LLC
Chambersburg PA
CBHW030341170426
43202CB00010B/1195